*The Renaissance Imagination
Important Literary and Theatrical Texts
from the Late Middle Ages
through the Seventeenth Century*

Stephen Orgel
Editor

Robert Carr and Frances Howard, the Earl and Countess of Somerset

THE TRUE TRAGICOMEDY FORMERLY ACTED AT COURT

A Play by Francis Osborne

Transcribed from the Manuscript
in the British Library
by John Pitcher and Lois Potter

edited, with an introduction, by
Lois Potter

The Renaissance Imagination
Volume 3

GARLAND PUBLISHING, INC.
NEW YORK & LONDON
1983

Copyright © 1983 by John Pitcher and Lois Potter
All rights reserved

Library of Congress Cataloging in Publication Data

Osborne, Francis, 1593–1659.
  The true tragicomedy formerly acted at court.

  (The Renaissance imagination ; v. 3)
  Includes bibliographical references and index.
  1. Great Britain—History—James I, 1603–1625—
Drama.   I. Pitcher, John.   II. Potter, Lois.
III. Title.   IV. Series.
PR3607.O82T7   1983   822'.4   80-9005
ISBN 0-8240-9403-4

Printed on acid-free, 250-year-life paper
Manufactured in the United States of America

CONTENTS

INTRODUCTION
    The Manuscript   i
    The Author   ii
    Osborne's Literary Career   xiii
    The Play   xvi
    The Essex Divorce   xx
    The Sources of the Play   xxiii
    The Play as Tragicomedy   xxxii
    This Edition   xxxvi
    Bibliographical Note   xxxviii

THE TEXT
    To the Reader   3
    The True Tragicomedy   40

APPENDIX
    A Biographical Dictionary of
    Characters Appearing or Mentioned
    in Osborne's Text   129

INTRODUCTION

The Manuscript

The True Tragicomedy exists in a single manuscript (Add MS 25348) in the British Library. It consists of 46 numbered sheets, of which the first 18 are taken up by the author's preface and a series of character sketches of well-known seventeenth-century figures, most of whom appear in the play. Bound in at the back of the play is a fragment of an indenture which presumably was once used as the cover for the manuscript; according to Mr. Hilton Kelliher, of the Department of Manuscripts, this comes from a copy (probably one of many) of the treaty by which Charles I was enabled to annex private lands to form Richmond New Park in 1635.

The manuscript is written in a hand which several scholars have agreed in describing as mid-seventeenth century (see plate 1). Internal evidence, however, makes it possible to be more precise. Bernard Wagner pointed out in 1928 that the reference on p.37 to a letter published in the second part of the Cabala (1654) effectively fixes the earliest date by which the MS might have been completed (though it is to be noted that the characters were written later than the play itself, as the author explains on page 3). Wagner's note is only a short one; he promised to discuss the play at more length later, but apparently never did. Its chief interest, for him and for others who have noticed it, was the reference to Jonson's Sejanus on p.4. He deduced that the author of The True Tragicomedy had been 'a man about town and had closely followed the events of court and city, of which his memory extended backward to almost the beginning of the century."[1]

---

1. Bernard M. Wagner, 'A Jonson Allusion, and Others', Philological Quarterly, VII (1928), p.307. See also the references in Ben Jonson, ed. C.H.Herford and Percy and Evelyn Simpson, 11 vols. (Oxford, 1925-52), Vol. IX, p.191, and G.E.Bentley, Jacobean and Caroline Stage, 7 vols. (Oxford, 1941-68), Vol.V, pp.1424-25.

The Author

What gives both the play and the characters their particular interest is the fact that the author claims on the title page to have been an eye-witness of the events he is describing. He refers to his personal experiences (particularly to the way he has been treated by members of his family); mentions other works of his ('my papers entitled my Memoirs'--p. 14); says that he was one of the audience which hissed <u>Sejanus</u>, presumably at its first performance in 1603; supplements the text with marginal notes elaborating on his references; and drops the names of other well-known figures whom he claims to have seen or heard in person(Bacon, Northampton, Coke) as well as events at which he was present, such as Lennox's practical joke (p. 29). With so many clues, it certainly ought to be possible to identify the author, and thus to assess the truth of his claim to first-hand knowledge.

As will be seen later, the author relies for his information mainly on histories and collections of correspondence published between 1649 and 1653. There is, however, one historian of this period from whom his borrowings are too close to be coincidence, and whose style is unmistakably the same as his. This is Francis Osborne, best known as the author of <u>Advice to a Son</u> (1655 and 1658) and <u>Historical Memoirs on the Reigns of Queen Elizabeth and King James</u> (1658). The conjunction of the stylistic resemblance with the biographical parallels which I shall explain shortly is so conclusive that I see no reason to labor it; most parallels between the play and Osborne's other works can best be made in footnotes to the text. However, it might be useful at this point to cite two examples. The first is Overbury's reply to Somerset, who has just argued that if everyone shared his friend's misogynistic views the world would soon be unpopulated:

> Let men of empty souls fill it, who can farm out their strength for bread and consume the labor of their land in making provision for the effects of another's lust, we having a weaker title to our heirs than to the curls of our hairs or parings of our nails, they being equal effects of an unnecessary redundancy in relation to individuals... a brother carrying more of our blood in him than a child, always a stranger on the surer side. (IV, iii,85-92, 96-8).

Introduction   iii

This can be compared with a passage from the most controversial section of <u>Advice to a Son</u>, that dealing with love and marriage:
> And if we consult right Reason, not Opinion, more of our Blood runs in a Brother than a Child; the surer side being always a stranger to the Family; the truth is, they are really no more ours, than the curles of our Hair, or the parings of our Nails, carrying often such thought towards us, as we should detest any for, but them.
> (Pt I. II. 25).

   More interesting than these verbal parallels are the passages which show that Osborne and the author of the play shared the same information, or misinformation. For instance, both of them describe the Earl of Northampton as brother to the Earl of Suffolk, whereas in fact he was the latter's uncle. A more tantalizing example is Northampton's comment on William Earl of Pembroke: 'he hath drawn his own process, by writing letters and bawdy verses to one the law makes it treason to solicit, though connived at in his age, where the distaff appeared more prevalent than the scepter.' (III, ii, 65-70). In <u>Advice to a Son,</u> Osborne refers to Pembroke, but without naming him: 'Let nothing unjustifiable or dangerous appear under your Hand, which many Years after, may rise up in Judgment against you, when things spoken may be forgot; as happened to the Duke of Norfolk, Sir Gervase Elvis[ie. Helwys], and a great Earl I knew led by the Nose all King James his Reign, for fear of being questioned about Letters writ to so high a Person as is Treason by the Law, to Solicite, &c.' (Part I, IV, 23).
   In 1660 a collection of poems by Pembroke, Rudyerd and others was published, edited by John Donne (the poet's son), who says that he got many of them from Christiana, Duchess of Devonshire; even at that date, the editor did not consider all of them suitable for printing. As a one-time member of the Pembroke household, Osborne might have known of the existence of other youthful indiscretions.
   While it is conceivable that a hack with a commonplace book might have accumulated some of the material in the <u>True Tragicomedy</u>, either from Osborne's published works or from one of the latter's sources, it is unlikely that such a writer could have assimilated his style so thoroughly. It is extremely distinctive in its piling up of participial clauses, its tendency to leave out relative pronouns, its digressive approach and correspondingly loose sentence structure, and its

tendency to end sentences with '&c', either out of laziness or to indicate that what follows is best left to the imagination.

It is, moreover, possible to correlate the autobiographical information given in the play's preface with that found in Osborne's other writings. There are two points which stand out in the playwright's account of himself. First, he claims that his motive for writing is that 'I have no better way to take my imagination off from poring upon my misfortunes than by letting it run a wool-gathering' (p.5). Second, at the end of his preface, he gives some hint of what these misfortunes were:

> If this be looked upon as too green a
> subject to creep from under so crazed
> and dried a roof, I refer them for an
> answer to that wise Italian, who urgeth
> it as an argument to the strength and
> integrity of his understanding that,
> being many years my senior, he had writ
> a comedy, nor can it be looked upon by
> me for less than an effect of Providence,
> that I should be entire in body and mind,
> when he that loaded me with misery died
> mad and rotten leaving (notwithstanding
> the vast revenue our father gave him)
> as distracted an estate to his issue, as
> his wife's covetousness and his own hath
> allotted for his two younger brethren,
> and their poor children. (p.39).

This obvious reference to some real or supposed wrong done him by an elder brother can be compared with a passage which occurs early in the Advice:

> Let not the *Titles of Consanguinity* betray
> you into a prejudiciall Trust: no blood
> being apter to raise a Fever, or cause a
> Consumption sooner in your poore Estate,
> then that which is nearest your owne; as
> I have most unhappily found, and your
> good Grandfather presaged, though God
> was pleased to leave it in none of our
> powers to prevent: nothing being truer
> in all *Solomon's* Observations, then that
> *A good Friend is neerer than an unnaturall
> Brother.* (Pt 1, I, 30).

Introduction

The Epistle to the Reader, which precedes the <u>Historical Memoirs</u>, is still more specific:

> *For after the* death *of a good* Father, *being driven into a corner of the world by* Injuries *received from* the nearest of Kindred, and remotest of Friends, *I was not onely invited by* Leisure, *but compell'd through* Necessity *to seek these* Diversions...

And the preface to his last published work, the <u>Miscellany</u> of 1659, echoes the rather self-congratulatory conclusion of the preface to the play:

> *...I have hitherto not onely been blest beyond my* Desert, *but* Expectation. *And have seen my* unnatural Oppressours *perish, and languish, through as* Miraculous *means, as I have been* Preserved. *And by which, I am brought to the* Contemplation *of* higher, *and more* permanent Pleasures, *then* the poor and despicable Consideration *of* Profit *is able to reach.*

The reasons for the frequent expressions of bitterness and disillusionment in his writings are not clear from the account of his life in the Dictionary of National Biography. This, like most of what has been written on Osborne, is based on Anthony à Wood's account in <u>Athenae Oxoniensis</u>(1691). Wood certainly knew something about Osborne, or at least about his publisher, but his description of him as 'an old atheistical courtier' does not suggest close acquaintance. His short biography was the basis of the anonymous one in the two-volume edition of Osborne's works published in 1722. The biographer does not seem well informed about the events of Osborne's time, and it seems likely that his main purpose was to enhance the importance of his author, since the edition is rather grandly titled <u>The Miscellaneous Works of that Eminent Statesman, Francis Osborn</u>. He reprints most of the personal letters of the 1659 <u>Miscellany</u> and also some interesting ones, not found elsewhere, which he says he received from the vicar of Nether Worton, the village where Osborne is buried. Unfortunately, neither the originals of these letters, nor anything else in Osborne's handwriting, appear to have survived. However, in the course of their research on Osborne's more famous niece Dorothy, both E.A.Parry and G.C. Moore-Smith came across information which makes it possible both to explain the precise nature of the writer's grievance and to give a fuller account of his life than has previously been available.

Francis Osborne or Osborn[1] was the youngest of the five sons of Sir John Osborne (1552-1628), a well-to-do court official who held posts in the Exchequer and was King's Remembrancer under both Elizabeth I and James I. He owned a house in London, where the family resided for much of the year, but his estate was at Chicksands Priory in Bedfordshire; in the latter part of his life he also acquired a manor house and farm at North Fambridge, Essex. His eldest son, Sir Peter Osborne, succeeded to the court offices as well as to the estates in London and Bedfordshire; the four younger sons received the North Fambridge manor as their inheritance. Sir Peter attended Oxford, but Francis, for some reason, never received any formal education. In the opening paragraph of <u>Advice to a Son</u>, he suggests that this was due to his father's indulgence; elsewhere, he describes himself as *'being from my* Birth,*uncapable to receive the Rich* Talent *of* Learning, *look'd upon, as* The onely Key of Knowledge: *which if obtayned had been Little Advantage, since I want a* Memory, *wherein to* Hoord *up what I had* stollen'.[2] His lack of university education seems to have left Francis both with a sense of diffidence about his own ability and with a good deal of contempt for mere scholars. Comparing Charles I, whose writings he admired, with the pedant James I, he concludes that *'Experience is a better Tutor then* Buchanan' (<u>Advice</u>, Pt.I, I,16). Rudyerd's rebuke of Overbury in IV,ii, shows a similar attitude.

His father's employment probably meant that Osborne spent most of his childhood in London, where it would have been possible for him (at the age of 10) to witness the first performance of <u>Sejanus</u> and, presumably at a later period, to attend sessions of Star Chamber. In his <u>Traditional Memoirs on the Reign of King James</u>, he gives an account of some of the other ways in which he spent his time:

> It was the fashion of those times...
> for the principall Gentry, Lords,
> Courtiers and men of all professions
> not meerely Mechanick, to meet in

---

1. He seems to have preferred Osborn, but most later references to him use the other spelling.
2. Preface to <u>Miscellany</u> (1659).

Introduction   vii

> Pauls Church by eleven, and walk in the
> middle Ile till twelve, and after dinner
> from three to six; during which time
> some discoursed of Businesse, others of
> Newes. Now, in regard to the universall
> commerce, there happened little that did
> not first or last arrive here: And I be-
> ing young, and wanting a more advantagious
> imployment, did, during my aboad in London,
> which was three fourth parts of the yeare,
> associate my selfe at those hours with the
> choycest company I could pick out, amongst
> such as I found most inquisitive after
> affaires of State; who being then my
> selfe in a daily attendance upon a hope
> (though a rotten one) of a future Prefer-
> ment, I appeared the more considerable,
> being as ready to satisfy, according to
> my weak abilities, their Curiosity, as
> they were mine. (para.20).

He also mentions that he used to manage an advance peep at the scenery for the court masques, though he regarded attending them as a waste of time and money. During the quarter of the year when he was out of London, he was probably at his father's country estate at Chicksands. He may have travelled abroad in his late teens, since that was the appropriate age to do so, and he occasionally refers to having learned something 'beyond sea' (eg., in Memoirs of King James, para.10) or 'the other side of the water'(Memoirs of Queen Elizabeth, para.12). He also admits that he was 'not near the English Court' at the time when Overbury had his greatest influence on Robert Carr--that is, 1610-12.[1] He may have been travelling then, or he may already have been living in the house of William Earl of Pembroke, whose master of the horse he is said to have been.[2]

At any rate, he was a member of that household in the 1620s, as is evidenced by some of the letters published in his Miscellany of 1659. His feelings about the Pembroke brothers (best known to literary scholars as successive holders of the office of Lord Chamberlain, patrons of the King's Men, and joint dedicatees of the first Shakespeare Folio) are

---

1. 'It is the Condition of those in Power to be guided by Servants' from Miscellany(1659), p.256.
2. Anthony à Wood, Athenae Oxoniensis,I,p.706.

similar to those of his contemporaries: he refers to William with some respect, though not so much as many of his fellow-historians, and seems to have shared the universal contempt for Philip, Earl of Montgomery, who became the fourth Earl of Pembroke. But it would appear that neither brother fulfilled his 'hope...of future preferment'. One of his letters from this period reads like a comment on his situation:

> *Honourable Persons,* like *too great Fires,* may *warm* and *comfort* such as are Content only to *serve* them at a Distance: But *blast* the *Parts,* and *consume* the *Fortunes* of those are found to *attend* them in any *neerer relations.* ...I remain in so high a *Feud* with *Greatnesse,* as, if I did not find [Lord] in my *Daily Prayers,* I should not *name* it (in relation to *Servant*) without *Detestation.*   1.

It seems likely, then, that his father's death in 1628, and perhaps the death of the third Earl in 1630, put an end to Osborne's ambitions of public office.

Osborne's subsequent career is hard to follow. From what he says in Advice, one should deduce that he had had some contact with major political figures, but his most recent biographer can find no trace of him before 1641, when, according to Anthony à Wood, he 'ran with the times'. It is hardly surprising that he accepted employment under Parliament, since the Pembroke brothers had both been known for their Puritan sympathies and the Fourth Earl took the side of Parliament at the outbreak of the war. Francis's political views are informed by a high degree of cynicism about both parties: he had a theoretical preference for republican rather than monarchical government, but despised the 'multitude'; he had little good to say of James I but shared the general admiration for Charles I, at least after his execution; his religious preferences were anglican rather than puritan, and he regarded the banning of public theatrical performances as a mistake. At several points in Advice, he stresses the dangers of excessive idealism and the need to temporize:

---

1. This is printed in the 1659 Miscellany(pp.153-6)as the second of two letters 'to Mr. W.P.'; the brackets are presumably those of the editor of the first edition.

Introduction

> That it is not unlawfull to Serve, bear
> Office or Armes under such as ascēd the
> Throne, or other high places, by Steps
> washed in blood, you may be abũdantly
> satisfied in Conscience, by the *Church*
> in *Neros House,* the good *Centuriõ,* &
> many others mentioned in Scripture.
> (Pt 1, IV, 19)

At some point in the 1630s, he married Anna Draper, by whom he had a son and three daughters. What little he says about his wife in the Advice is affectionate, as is his later dedication of the Miscellany to his niece; his theoretical misogyny, which one critic has described as 'little more than pathological',[1] probably had little influence on his practical conduct. Similarly, though he condemns Philip Earl of Pembroke for the 'passion against Learning' that he displayed during the Visitation of Oxford,[2] he was quite prepared to profit by the fact that his brother-in-law, William Draper, was a colonel in the Parliamentary army and one of the Visitors. The object of the Visitation was to eject from their scholarships and fellowships all members of the University who still supported episcopacy. It was thanks to Draper that Osborne's son John was admitted to Magdalen College in 1648 and, in 1651, was awarded a fellowship at All Souls,[3] where he remained until 1654.

During at least part of this time, Osborne must have been living in Oxford or at his brother-in-law's estate at Nether Worton, only ten miles from there. According to Wood, he was one of a seven-man commission who dealt with prisoners in the city and county: an appointment which he probably owed to Draper. He obviously found Oxford congenial. Some of the Gresham College circle, the nucleus of the future Royal Society, had moved there after 1648. Many of his ideas

---

1. D.R.M. Wilkinson, The Comedy of Habit (Leiden, 1964),p.39.
2. Memoirs of King James, para.23.
3. E.A.Parry gives a fuller account of the circumstances of this award in the introduction to his edition of Advice to a Son (London, 1896), pp.xvi-xix, which supplements and corrects Wood's account in Athenae Oxoniensis.

reflect the influence of this group: his admiration for such men as Ralegh, Bacon, Browne, and Hobbes;[1] his stress on the importance of mathematics;[2] his ridicule of the notorious controversialist Alexander Ross for his inveterate hostility to any new idea.[3] According to Aubrey, Hobbes (who returned to England from the Continent in 1651) was 'his great acquaintance.'[4]

John Osborne went on from Oxford to the Inner Temple in 1654, and had a successful legal career. It was for him that Osborne wrote his Advice. Its tone of disillusionment, as well as its frequent reminders that John will have to make the best of straitened circumstances, are the result of the other major event of these years.

In a document of 1652 Osborne is referred to as residing at North Fambridge, the family's Essex estate, which had been left to the younger sons in Sir John Osborne's will of 1628. Two of Francis's brothers died without issue in the 1630s; a third, Thomas, died in 1651, leaving two sons. While Francis had been serving the Parliamentary cause, in however unpretentious a capacity, his older brother, Sir Peter, had been fighting on the King's party. He had been stationed at Cornet Castle, Guernsey, since 1627, when there had been fear of a French invasion; during the Civil War, when the rest of the island declared for Parliament, he continued to hold the castle until he gave up its governorship in 1646. In 1649 he had to compound for delinquency: that is, to pay a fine in order to retain his estates, otherwise forfeit because he had fought against Parliament. The once-flourishing Osborne fortunes were now in danger, and Sir Peter's younger brothers were alarmed at his attempt to compound for the North Fambridge estate with the rest of his property. From this point on, its ownership was hotly contested. What finally made Francis take the case to court was the fact that Sir Peter handed the estate over to his son Henry, who began evicting some of Francis's tenants in 1652. Full details of the lawsuit, and transcripts of some of the documents, can be found in Appendix IX of G.C.Moore-Smith's edition of the letters of Dorothy Osborne. It is sufficient

---

1. See the addresses to the reader in Advice, Pt 1, and the Miscellany.
2. Advice, Pt 1, 1,7.
3. 'To the Reader', Miscellany.
4. Brief Lives, ed. Andrew Clark, 2 Vols (Oxford, 1898), I, p.370.

Introduction   xi

to know that the action was decided in Henry Osborne's favour
in 1653, that Francis appealed, and that the end finally came
in March 1655, with a verdict in favor of Henry. By now,
Francis was the only surviving Osborne brother. Sir Peter
himself had died in 1654 after an illness which lasted about
a year; Moore-Smith notes that his signature on a document
of 9 February 1653 is written 'in a very shaky hand'.[1]
Francis's reference in TT to his oppressor having died 'mad
and rotten', and to 'his two younger brethren, and their poor
children' (only Francis and Thomas had children), as well as
to the 'distracted estate' (Henry's subsequent career was a
series of lawsuits, including one with his sister Dorothy)
coincide at too many points with the circumstances of this
case to leave any doubt as to their connection. It is hardly
surprising that Francis's description of Sir Peter hardly re-
sembles Dorothy Osborne's view of him as 'the best Father in
the world'.[2]

   It is not clear whether the two brothers and their
families ever met anywhere except in the courtroom. The difference in their political convictions would not have been a
barrier, since Sir Peter's wife was a member of the Danvers
family, which included both dedicated Royalists and a distinguished regicide. Dorothy's letters to Temple never mention either Francis or the lawsuit, though it was drawing to
its end at the time of their courtship. It is not impossible,
however, that he was on friendly terms with her and her family before 1652. An undated letter in the Miscellany might
perhaps have been addressed to her. She herself says that she
used to describe her ideal of matrimony in such inflated terms
that young men had 'a Custome of Expressing any thing that is
noe where but in fiction by the name of Mrs. O's husband.'[3]
Osborne's letter, which is headed *A letter persuading _____
to marry,* harps on both these points:

> If you resolve upon none, till you pattern
> the Character your Fancy presented to me,
> (when I had last the Honor to kisse your
> *hands,* and heard the Scorn wherewith you

---

1. Letters of Dorothy Osborne, Appendix IX, p.316; see also
   Letter 17,n.1, p.227.
2. Ibid., Letter 61, p.155.
3. Ibid., Letter 71, p.174 (slightly modernized).

> received the Offer of _____ I
> must be bold to tell you, I took it
> rather as a *Copy* of your *Countenance*,
> then any thought could take its
> *Originall* from the *Discretion* I ever
> own'd you *Lady of*) you may as well
> expect a *New Creation*. Since, so
> much perfection as your Language did
> then paynt, is not to be found out
> of a *Romance*... (<u>Miscellany</u>,p.164).

It has been pointed out that an anecdote which occurs in his <u>Advice</u> can also be found in one of her letters to Temple,[1] and one of Temple's biographers has noted parallels between his works and those of his uncle-by-marriage.[2] However, the only niece toward whom Osborne expressed fondness on paper is his brother-in-law's daughter Elizabeth who eventually married John Osborne. His dedication of several of his works to his 'brother Draper', and of the <u>Miscellany</u> to Elizabeth, may have been a way of indicating his total rejection of his 'real' brother and his brother's family as well.

The failure of the lawsuit must have been financially ruinous. Some of Osborne's letters of the 1650s are dated from Kelvedon in Essex, which is perhaps the 'corner of the world' to which he describes himself as having been driven. After the death of his wife in 1657 he sold his property to pay his debts and wrote to Draper that he was going to return to Nether Worton, 'presuming, if I should prove intolerable to you, I were not far from that place [Oxford] I am confident I can live in with as much Content as my age and condition is capable of'.[3] He seems to have spent the rest of his life as a guest of others, both at Nether Worton and at Oxford, where he stayed with his publisher Robinson. By now he was suffering from 'the stone', and it is evident from his preface to the <u>Traditional Memoirs of King James</u> that he was expecting death,'*that fatall Sub-poena we are all liable to through our fathers concupiscence, no lesse then a reciprocall necessity to leave elbow-roome for our own*'. He died in February 1659, at the house of his brother-

---

1. <u>Ibid</u>., Letter 56, n., p.271. Cf.<u>Advice</u>, Pt 1, III, 21.
2. Homer E. Woodbridge, <u>Sir William Temple, the Man and His Work</u> (New York and London, 1940),pp.287-88 and p.294, n.
3. Printed in the 1722 edition of his works (I, pp.14-15) and in Parry's edition of <u>Advice to a Son,</u> p. xxv.

Introduction

in-law. An epitaph of his own composition is printed in the Miscellany. Like all his verse, it is unremarkable.

Osborne's Literary Career

As we have seen, Osborne consistently described his writings as the product of idleness and depression, and the one mitigating circumstance of his last years must have been the surprising success of Advice to a Son, which turned him into a literary celebrity. He had clearly been writing for some time. The Miscellany (1659) is a rag-bag of works, mostly from the pre-war years: poems, letters, paradoxes, character sketches, essays. Many are unfinished, or look like first drafts. They show that Osborne, though his ideas are often strikingly original, preferred to work within familiar genres and on topical issues, usually taking other writers' work as his point of departure. He was really a sort of literary journalist.

His two earliest publications, as far as is known, appeared anonymously in 1652. There is a mysterious reference in the Miscellany which may apply to these works or to others not now known:

> there hath been from the beginning of the *uncivil wars* (wherein none were *masters* of what they had) diverse *imperfect Copies* of my own hand left in the custody of one did Print some of them, under a *nameless author* though very false, And might have done this, if not timely prevented. 1.

The first of these, A Persuasive to a Mutual Compliance under the Present Government (Feb.1652), is his contribution to the Engagement controversy, which had already been going on for some years.[2] It reads like a plea for attention,and perhaps for public office: he expresses himself as willing to serve the new government, and asks Cromwell to take Oxford under his protection. Coupled with it is A Plea for a Free State Compared with Monarchy,which expresses a characteristic view(cf. James I's remarks in II,V,i) that hereditary monarchy is an unsafe principle because it 'is made so contingent,by the infidelity of women'(p.5). A Seasonable

---

1. 'Deductions from the History of the Earl of Essex', Miscellany,pp.227-8.
2. See J.M.Wallace,'The Engagement Controversy of 1649-1652. an Annotated List of Pamphlets', Bulletin of the New York Public Library 68 (1964),pp.384-405.

Expostulation with the Netherlands (June 1652) reminds the Dutch that they have no cause to blame the English, since they themselves once rebelled against a ruler no worse than Charles. Neither of these pamphlets is included in Osborne's collected works, perhaps because he came to regard them as too radical (the Persuasive even suggests that some of the Levellers' proposals deserve attention). The Expostulation takes a much harsher tone towards Charles I than is found elsewhere in Osborne's writings; he sums him up as 'a better Man than a King'.

Both the Expostulation and the Plea for a Free State may have been inspired by the republication in 1651 of Observations on the Provinces United and on the State of France, a work attributed to Sir Thomas Overbury and containing a parallel between the Dutch republic and the French monarchy. Osborne says himself that he wrote his essay, 'Deductions from the History of the Earl of Essex' (published in the Miscellany), in answer to Sir Henry Wotton's parallel between Essex and the Duke of Buckingham, which at the time he knew only as a manuscript said to be in circulation among Wotton's friends.[1] Similarly, the work which made him famous, Advice to a Son, follows not long after reprints of works in the same genre by Burghley and Ralegh. It was first published anonymously in 1655, perhaps for fear of embarrassing his son. Its success was very rapid: according to Wood, it went through several editions in the next two years, and created a demand for more works by the same author. Osborne obliged by giving his publisher a collection of essays on such subjects as the government of the Turks and a defence of Machiavelli,[2] which were published in 1656 as 'By the Author of the Late Advice to a Son'. They naturally enhanced his reputation for cynicism and atheism. The translator of a Dialogue of Polygamy (1657) dedicated it to the still-anonymous author of the Advice, on the grounds that the latter was clearly 'ingenious and free-spirited, of the temper so much (and that deservedly) magnified by Charron [the French Stoic philosopher] as a principal accomplishment

---

1. Pp. 234-5 and 239. Wotton's parallel was first published in 1641.
2. These were also topical subjects: the first English translations of The Prince and the Koran had been published in 1640 and 1649 respectively.

Introduction   xv

of the Wise-Man'. It was a somewhat embarrassing tribute,
and no doubt had something to do with the unsuccessful attempt of Oxford authorities to prevent booksellers from selling the Advice because, according to Wood, it was thought
to 'instill principles of atheism' into young scholars.
   When Part Two of Advice to a Son was published in 1658,
along with an enlarged re-issue of Part One, it had Osborne's
name on the title page. The result was further notoriety.
On a visit to London, he wrote to Draper, 'I am become a
Prodigy, and if my Picture were drawn, might possibly drop
Pence with a Puppet-Play. The truth is, many desire my Company, which I out of Tediousness or Discretion avoid.'[1] For
no better reason than a desire to cash in on the success of
Osborne's work, a hack astrologer and amateur Rosicrucian
named John Heydon attacked him as 'thou Relique of a Polit-
ician' in his Advice to a Daughter (1658). Heydon was at
once attacked in return by another hack, the young law stu-
dent Thomas Pecke, in Advice to Balaam's Ass. Pecke pointed
out that Heydon's book was a tissue of absurd accusations
and plagiarisms and urged him to 'prostrate yourself in an
ingenious Recantation, at the feet of Grave, and Learned
Mr. *Osborn*.' To judge from the tone in which Osborne refers
to the episode in the preface of his Miscellany, it was of
no great concern to him.
   The Historical Memoirs, also published in 1658, were obviously influenced by the spate of historical writings that,
after 1649,looked back to the earlier decades of the century
with the aid of hindsight. Osborne seems to have thought
rather well of them, though he occasionally shows his aware-
ness of their tendency to ramble. But they are incomplete:
the Memoirs of James's reign break off with the comment that
'my pen is stopped through indisposition' before he has
reached the events which constitute the subject matter of The
True Tragicomedy. They often read like first drafts,which
is probably what they are. It is possible that Part One of
Advice to a Son benefitted from the attentions of an editor--
perhaps Robinson, or the Mr. Wood whom Osborne, in a letter,
describes as his 'midwife'.[2] The lack of any such editorial
hand is evident in the works published in 1658 and after,
which were obviously rushed into print to take advantage of
Osborne's sudden popularity. He must have turned all his

---

1. Letter VIII, in Works (1722), I, p.24.
2. Ibid, p.25.

papers over to the publisher, including many which he rightly describes as 'waste paper'.

The Play

Probably the reason for the disappearance of Osborne's other manuscripts is that the printing house destroyed them after they had been used as the basis of the first editions of his works. This would suggest that The True Tragicomedy was not among the manuscripts given by Osborne to his printer. It is, of course, highly unlikely that any stationer would have been willing to risk the publication of a work guaranteed to offend readers of every political party. Its depiction of James I is particularly scandalous: not only does Osborne repeat all the familiar descriptions of his unsavory behavior, he puts explicitly machiavellian language into the king's mouth and makes him argue in favor of homosexuality as a means of ensuring a low birth rate and a higher standard of living. But Osborne also makes some rather flippant remarks about the misfortune of James's daughter Elizabeth and her large family; he ridicules Essex, who was to become a respected leader of the Parliamentary army, and is equally harsh about Cromwell (see II,ii, 27-28). Osborne says at the end of his preface that he does not intend the work for publication, and this is probably truer than his other disclaimers of the same kind.

If the earliest possible date for the preface is, as Professor Wagner said, 1655, the latest must be September 1658, since it is difficult to imagine so topical a writer failing to mention the death of Cromwell. Of the play itself we know only that it was written before the preface, but there seems no reason to doubt that the two date from the same period, and there is some corroboration in Osborne's use of material from Wilson's History of Great Britain (1653) for the Lennox subplot. If the reference to his Memoirs on p.14 means, as seems likely, his Historical Memoirs, I should guess that these had been written but not yet published at the time Osborne was writing the preface. The Memoirs frequently drop hints of the Carr story, 'but', Osborne adds at one point, 'there appears so many leaves lying between his advancement and ruine, as I am not at this time prepared to remove.' (para.30) Perhaps, after breaking off his memoirs of James's reign, he decided to continue them in a different form.

In one respect, at least, The True Tragicomedy makes no concessions to dramatic form. All the characters speak in the same style--there is no attempt, for instance, to reproduce the Scots speech of James, Carr, or Lennox, though

Introduction

Mrs. Turner said at her trial that Carr's accent was so strong that she was unable to understand him. If Osborne set out with the idea of writing the play in verse, he soon gave up the attempt. The alternation of verse and prose is used effectively in James's opening speech and gives some stature to Northampton in his final appearance. Verse also helped Osborne to control his rambling syntax, and at times the lineation of the prose speeches appears to be a substitute for punctuation. But essentially the style is that of his other works.

This style has always provoked mixed reactions. It was unkindly described by a critic in 1912:

> all the faults, and none of the virtues, of the older prose...a strange admixture of platitude and paradox... The style, when it is not terse and apophthegmatic, as of one trying to imitate Bacon, is stiff with conceits and longwinded sentences. 1.

Even in the eighteenth century, critics were divided about the gossipy, digressive manner which delighted Oxford undergraduates in the 1650s. Swift grouped Osborne with Wotton, Naunton, and Daniel, as courtiers who used such a fashionable style that now 'they are often not to be understood, or appear perfectly ridiculous.'[2] Boswell, who, in 1772, considered publishing an edition of the Advice, found that Johnson did not share his enthusiasm for it:

> I expressed a liking for Mr. Francis Osborne's works, and asked him what he thought of that writer. He answered, 'A conceited fellow. Were a man to write so now, the boys would throw stones at him.' He, however, did not alter my opinion of a favourite author, to whom I was first directed by his being quoted in The Spectator, and in

---

1. A.A.Tilley, 'The Essay and the Beginning of Modern English Prose', in The Cambridge History of English Literature, Vol VIII, p.377.
2. The Tatler, No.230 (Sept.26-28,1710).

> whom I have found much shrewd and lively
> sense, expressed indeed in a style some-
> what quaint, which, however, I do not
> dislike. His book has an air of originality.
> We figure to ourselves an ancient gentleman
> talking to us. 1.

Douglas Bush, in 1945, found other qualities to praise, describing the style as 'pungently independent' and the author
as 'hard-boiled'.[2] Such other comment as I have seen on
Osborne's writing has concentrated mainly on his cynicism and
the extent to which it is an expression of his age.[3] Both the
play and the preface will probably give rise to the same range
of response. The passages which seem to have been most care-
fully worked over, such as the Character of the Countess of
Hertford, show that Osborne was capable of writing with grace
and wit, but the work has all the faults of a first draft,
and it cannot be claimed that it is anything more than this.

The fact that the Characters take up nearly as much room
as the play perhaps indicates where the author's real interest lay. The story of Overbury might have given him the idea
of writing in this form, though Overbury's Characters, like
those which Osborne wrote in his youth,[4] were not about real
people but general types. His reason for writing a play
rather than another historical essay seems to have been sheer
caprice: 'a Frenchman said in my hearing there lived not an
Englishman able to digest this story into a comedy, much less
come near one of his countrymen who had done it already,
though not published...'

---

1. Life of Johnson ed. I.F.Powell and Birkbeck Hill (Oxford, etc., 1904,1961)pp.133,147; cf. Boswell for the Defence, ed. W.K.Wimsatt and F.A.Pottle,(New Haven, 1960), where Boswell describes making notes on the Advice.
2. English Literature of the Early Seventeenth Century(Oxford, 1945), p.23, p.25.
3. Eg., the introduction to Advice to a Son by Louis B.Wright (Ithaca, NY., 1962), p.xxvi; Siegmund A.E.Betz, 'Francis Osborne's "Advice to a Son"', in Seventeenth Century Studies ed. R.Shafer,2nd series (Princeton, etc., 1937), pp.3-67; Royce Macgillivray, Restoration Historians and the English Civil War (The Hague, 1974) p.29
4. 'Honour', 'Valour and Cowardice', 'a Debauched Soldier', 'a Cook', and 'a Host' (all published in the 1659 Miscellany).

Introduction   xix

Though I have not been able to find the Frenchman's play,
the story suggests that Osborne's may be less anomalous than
it seems. Scurrilous plays on topical themes, lampooning
real people, are known to have existed before 1642, but in
nearly every case they were so effectively suppressed that
we now know of them only through the legal proceedings to
which they usually gave rise.[1] The most obvious exception
is Middleton's Game at Chess (1624) which represented the
principal figures involved in the negotiations for Prince
Charles's Spanish marriage. Middleton had already made a
pretty explicit reference to Frances Howard's virginity test
in The Changeling (1622), which was first published in 1652
and may have been in Osborne's mind while he was writing
this play. Margot Heinemann has suggested that the character of Francisca in Middleton's The Witch (1616) may be a
still more topical reference to Lady Frances.[2] However,
none of these plays used real names, as Osborne does.

   The closing of the theatres in 1642 did not put a
stop to the writing of plays; if anything, it encouraged
the association between drama and a subversive attitude.
Osborne may have seen some of the curious miniature plays
that were published as pamphlets in the 1640s. The royalist
journalists writing between 1647 and 1649 responded to the
renewal of the ban on public performances by writing vicious
dramatic caricatures of the Parliamentary leaders (usually
called by their own names), which show a taste for sexual
intrigue (eg., the adulteries of Cromwell's and Fairfax's
wives) and supernatural effects.[3] Among the full-length
plays of the period it is possible to find both classical
closet dramas and works which would have lent themselves to
public performance on a stage of the pre-war type.

   It is evident that Osborne's model is popular rather
than closet drama. Stage directions like 'exit at one door
...enter at another' show that he was thinking of the conventional unlocalised stage; at one point (III,i) he calls

---

1. See, eg., C.J. Sisson, Lost Plays of Shakespeare's Age
   (Cambridge, 1936).

2. Puritanism and Theatre: Thomas Middleton and Opposition
   Drama under the Early Stuarts (Cambridge, etc., 1980),
   pp.107-111.

3. See my chapter on Civil War and Commonwealth Drama in Vol
   IV of The Revels History of Drama in English (London,1981).

for the drawing of a curtain for the purpose of a 'discovery'. Further 'popular' elements are the use of song, the boy disguised as a girl, the heroine who disguises herself as a prostitute, and the use of 'low' characters in a choric capacity (I, iii, and V, vi). The prevailing cynicism recalls Jonsonian tragedy, and the addition of footnotes may have been suggested to Osborne by the most frequently cited play of the 1650s, Jonson's Catiline;[1] a still more heavily annotated work, however, was Robert Baron's Mirza (1655), a closet drama modeled on Catiline and, like it, based on historical research. The Civil War and Commonwealth period was a time of experiment with mixed genres: F.H. Ristine has noted the number of plays of this period which describe themselves as tragicomedies.[2] Osborne's play is, however, a doubly mixed form, since it claims to be not only drama but history, not only tragicomic, but 'true'. To evaluate the justice of this claim, it is necessary first to look at its subject matter.

The Essex Divorce

The episode on which Osborne based his play had already been retold many times before 1655, and it continues to fascinate historians. A brief summary of events may be useful at this point.

In 1606 the young Earl of Essex and Lady Frances Howard were married, at the ages of fourteen and fifteen respectively. The father of Robert Devereux was the popular hero and favorite of Queen Elizabeth who was executed in 1601 for attempting to lead an uprising against her; Lady Frances's father, the Earl of Suffolk, had helped to put down that uprising and had sat as a commissioner at Essex's trial. The marriage was apparently meant as a means of reconciling the two families. After the wedding, Essex went off to travel on the Continent, returning late in 1609. Frances, who had been living at court, had meanwhile fallen in love with Robert Carr, a young Scot who was rising rapidly in the King's favor and hence in fortune. When Essex returned and became aware of the situation, he took her to his country house, Chartley. That she was desperately unhappy during this period is made clear in letters to her friend Anne

---

1. See G.E. Bentley, Shakespeare and Jonson, 2 Vols. (Chicago, 1945), I, pp.109-112.

2. English Tragicomedy, Its Origins and History (New York, 1910), pp.153-4.

Introduction   xxi

Turner, which were read out at her trial in 1616. Early
in 1613 she persuaded her family to investigate the possibility of annulling the marriage on the grounds that it
had never been consummated.
      By now, Carr had become Viscount Rochester, the first
Scot to sit in the House of Lords; he had been given the
estate of Sherborne (once Sir Walter Ralegh's, but forfeited because of an error in the drawing up of a legal
document); he had also been made a privy councillor, and
had recently taken on the role of unofficial secretary to
the King. Since he had hitherto been using his immense influence against the Howard family, they naturally welcomed
the opportunity to get him on their side. This was particularly true of Frances's great-uncle, the Earl of Northampton,
who had finally achieved some of his political ambitions
after years of frustration in Queen Elizabeth's reign, and
was now prepared to co-operate with anyone who could help
him achieve the rest. In May 1613 a preliminary meeting was
held between representatives of husband and wife, and a commission was set up to investigate the case. Since Essex
naturally wished to save his reputation and to be able to
remarry, the cause for divorce could not be simply impotence.
It was agreed that he should claim to have been the victim
of 'fascination' - or witchcraft - which, however, affected
him only in relation to Lady Frances. James was persuaded
to throw his influence behind this claim. An examination,or
'scrutiny', established the truth of Frances's claim that
she was still a virgin. She was allowed to keep her face
covered during the proceedings, a fact which soon gave rise
to speculation that someone else had been substituted for
her.
      Meanwhile, however, a further complication had arisen.
Carr's friend and adviser, Sir Thomas Overbury, had consistently advised him against the marriage with Lady Frances,
either because he distrusted her and her family, or because
he was afraid of their effect on his own position. He was a
threat not only because of his vociferous opposition but
also because of his intimate knowledge of all the details of
this shady business. Rochester and Northampton decided that
he must be got out of the way. Overbury was first offered a
post on the Continent, but refused it, He was then (on
April 21, 1613) committed to the Tower, on the grounds that
his refusal constituted contempt of the King's commands. As
the proceedings for the divorce went on, Overbury wrote increasingly desperate letters to Rochester, Suffolk and
Northampton. Among other things, he complained of ill health.
What exactly was happening during this period has been the
object of much historical detective work; it seems generally

agreed that Lady Frances was attempting, through a series of not very effective agents, to have Overbury poisoned. Whether Rochester and Northampton knew this is less clear.

Overbury died on September 15. The Essex divorce, or rather annulment, was granted ten days later by a majority of seven to five. Rochester became Earl of Somerset on November 3, and married Frances Howard on December 26. A number of observers commented on the fact that she wore her hair long, as a virgin bride. There is plenty of evidence of the grovelling flattery that this couple received at their marriage and in the course of the following year. But already Somerset's opponents were trying to undermine his position. George Villiers first met James in August 1614, and came to court in November. Through the influence of Queen Anne and the Archbishop of Canterbury (who had voted against the divorce), this handsome young man was made a gentleman of the bedchamber to the King in April 1615. Somerset's touchiness about this threatened rival contributed to the worsening of his own relations with James. In September of that year the Secretary of State, Sir Ralph Winwood, told the King of the rumors which had reached him about the poisoning of Overbury. The resultant trial, which dragged on until May of the following year, led to the deaths of many of the minor villains, including Mrs. Turner and the Lieutenant of the Tower. What aroused particular excitement was Frances's trial, at which her letters to the astrologer, Simon Forman, and some of the pictures and love charms which he had sold her, were displayed. She pleaded guilty. Somerset refused to do so, but was also found guilty. Unlike the humbler criminals, however, they were both pardoned, she in July 1616, he not until 1624. In 1622 they were released from the Tower.

A curious sequel to this affair occurred a few years later. In 1616 one of the other followers of the Howard family, Sir Thomas Lake, married his daughter Anne to William Cecil, Lord Roos, who was the great-grandson of Elizabeth I's most trusted statesman, Lord Burghley. Lord Roos had already travelled extensively, was known to prefer the Continent to England, and was also a committed homosexual. Anne and her family proceeded to blackmail him, holding over his head the prospect of another embarrassing divorce like Essex's. In 1617 he finally took the pretext of a journey to the north as an opportunity to flee to Italy, and died at Naples a year later. These are the bare outlines of a story which Osborne mentions several times, embroidered with the various rumors that accompanied it. The scandal got to the Star Chamber because, after Roos's flight, his wife decided

Introduction   xxiii

to accuse Lady Exeter (the young wife of his grandfather) of
having committed incest with Lord Roos and having tried to
poison her. The investigation of these charges, in which
the King took a prominent role, led to the exposure of Lady
Roos, who had suborned witnesses and forged letters in order
to make her case. In 1619 her family was ordered to pay a
substantial fine to Lady Exeter, and Sir Thomas Lake lost
his post as Secretary of State. The revelation of further
corruption in Suffolk's behaviour as Lord Treasurer, meanwhile, had led to his being fined and disgraced. Lord
Wallingford, the husband of Frances's sister Elizabeth, also
lost his post, for no real reason except that his wife, like
Suffolk's,was said to have too much influence over him. Other
members of the family were also dismissed from places at
court. As Chamberlain reported, in the first months of 1620,
'Our pulpits ring continually of the insolence and impudence
of women: and to helpe the matter forward the players have
likewise taken them to taske, and so to the ballades and
ballad singers, so that they can come no where but theyre
eares tingle.'[1]

    The Howards were not completely ruined, but they were
never again to be so politically powerful. As they fell,
Villiers and his family rose. He became Earl of Buckingham
(1617),then Marquis (1619) and Duke (1623). His supporters
soon realised that the new favorite was even worse than the
old. But by then it was too late.

    Frances died in 1632, Somerset in 1645; Essex married
again, but his second marriage ended in separation after his
wife was accused of adultery. When he became General of the
Parliamentary forces in 1642, royalist ballad-writers made
capital out of his past history: one said that a man with
horns could not fairly be described as a roundhead; another,
that his marital situation gave a new meaning to the word
'separatist'.[2]

The Sources of the Play

    The True Tragicomedy combines several plots: the Essex
divorce; the romantic subplot of Lennox and the Countess of
Hertford; the intrigues of Northampton with the Jesuits;
and, framing all these, James I's irresponsible handling of
events.

---

1. Letters, II, p.289.
2. A Collection of Poems and Ballads in ridicule of the Parliamentary Party during the Quarrel with Charles I
   (Huntington Library MS 16522),p.38 ,p.88.

For his choice, and his treatment, of this largely scandalous subject matter Osborne had several models. Essentially, there were two aspects to the process of reinterpreting the past which began almost immediately after the execution of Charles I. The first was a demystification of the image of the ruler and an increasing interest in the once-forbidden secrets of state--Arcana Imperii, King-Craft, etc.--which had been part of that mystification. James I had insisted that there were certain matters into which it was impudent, even unsafe, for ordinary eyes to peer; the analogy with divine mysteries was obvious. But the seizure of Charles I's private correspondence at the Battle of Naseby, and its publication in 1646, marked the end of this secrecy. Though Royalists professed themselves shocked at the intrusion into the King's privacy, they were quick to exploit the same device for propaganda purposes: Eikon Basilike, after all, purported to be a still more private view of Charles I, drawn from his prayers and meditations in prison. An enterprising publisher collected some sententiae from it and published them as Apopthegmata aurea in October 1649. It was the first of a number of collections of golden sayings: those of James I were published the following July.

Many collections of letters, both public and private, were published under the Commonwealth. The editor of Sir Henry Wotton's essays and letters promised the reader 'many observations of the Misteries and Laberinths in Courts and States',[1] while a miscellaneous collection of Tudor and Stuart tracts (which included Burghley's Advice to his Son) described them as 'Arcana Imperii'[2]. A two-part collection of state correspondence, which Osborne had clearly read before embarking on the characters in his preface, was published under the titles Cabala, or Mysteries of State(1653) and Scrinia Sacra (1654). Osborne himself used the fashionable phrase in his 'Political Reflections upon the Government of the Turks', where he speaks of the 'Turkish Arcana'.[3]

---

1. Reliquiae Wottonianae (1651), 'An Advertisement to the Reader'.
2. Francis Bacon, The Felicity of Queen Elizabeth and her Times etc. (1651),Preface.
3. See his Epistle to the Reader.

The facts revealed by these documents--for instance, the extent to which England had seemed to be flirting with Catholicism at the time of the Spanish marriage negotiations in 1623--shocked many readers. An appetite had been created for other revelations, more shocking yet. Rumors which for the most part had made their way only by word of mouth now found publishers. Royalists and Parliamentarians shared a common concern to explain the downfall of the House of Stuart.

Hence, the second aspect of Commonwealth historiography, the assimilation of the history of the House of Stuart to that of the House of Atreus, with Charles's errors (magnified by the Parliamentarians, minimized by the Royalists) largely lost in the contemplation of the far greater scandals of his father's court. The parallel was in fact made explicit within a few months of Charles I's execution, when the Royalist Christopher Wase published a translation of the Electra of Sophocles, with copious notes pointing out parallels with recent events. Other writers found historical parallels of a different kind. Sir Robert Cotton's History of the Reign of Henry III, which had shown the damage that can be done by foreign rule, royal favorites, and lavish but indiscriminate bounty, had been republished in 1642 along with Sir John Hayward's history of Henry IV, which, although it warned against the deposing of kings, also pointed out that 'these and the like accidents daily happen to such Princes as will bee absolute in power[,] resolute in will, and dissolute in life.'[1] In 1650 George Walker drew on Cotton's history for his Anglo-Tyrannus. Or the Idea of a Norman Monarch, represented in the paralell Reignes of Henrie the Third and Charles Kings of England.

Charles II's landing in Scotland in June 1650, and his unsuccessful invasion of England the following year, shifted attention more specifically to the House of Stuart: Marchamont Nedham devoted several numbers of the official news-sheet, Mercurius Politicus, to the discrediting of all members of that family, alive or dead. 1652 saw the publication both of a translation of a sixteenth-century attack on Mary Stuart by George Buchanan (first published in Latin) and of Sir Edward Peyton's Divine Catastrophe of the Kingly Family of the House of Stuarts, perhaps the most violent of all the attacks on that family. The anonymous A Cat May Look

---

1. The History of the Life and Raigne of King Henry the Fourth (1642 [first published 1599]), p.291.

upon a King (1653), though it has no good word for any monarch since the Norman conquest, traces the most recent events to one specific culprit:

> The unparallel'd Transactions of these our late times have raised in mee such a confusion of thoughts, that I resolved to look back; as a man that is stunn'd with a stone, looks not after the stone, but after the hand that flung it.
>
> And surely I find (by the help of my spectacles) King JAMES was the Fountain of all our late Afflictions and miseries. (pp.1-2)

Three important histories of James's reign were published in the years immediately preceeding the True Tragicomedy. Anthony Weldon's Court and Character of King James, probably written a good deal earlier, appeared in October 1650. William Sanderson's answer to it, Aulicus Coquinariae, dates from March 1651. Arthur Wilson's History of Great Britain, being the Life and Reign of King James the First (1653), attempts, according to the author, to steer a middle course between the 'court' and the 'kitchen'. An anonymous 'Lover of the Truth' also attacked Sanderson, in a pamphlet not published until 1656.[1] All these books naturally discuss the Overbury affair. Weldon goes so far as to make James, on first hearing of the accusations against Somerset, behave like a classical tragic hero: he tells the judges who are to investigate the charge, 'if you shall spare any guilty of this crime, Gods curse light on you and your posterity: and if I spare any that are found guilty, Gods curse light on me and my posterity, for ever!' James did of course pardon the Earl and Countess of Somerset, and Weldon goes on to suggest that the effects of this curse have been felt by the unfortunate Princess Elizabeth (the Queen of Bohemia) and by all the people of England.[2] Sanderson, in reply, attempts to defend James, partly by playing down the importance of the Overbury affair and claiming that the king did make every effort to see justice done; he also writes, surprisingly, at some length about the slightly later scandal of Lady Roos. Probably his intention was to balance the discreditable example of James's intervention in a legal process

---

1. Observations upon some particular persons and passages in a Book lately made publick.
2. Court and Character of King James, p.409.

Introduction

xxvii

with a story which showed him to better advantage. Two sensational accounts of the Overbury murder were also published in 1651, including some of the records of the trial.[1]

Osborne must also have looked at some accounts of another story which, like that of Overbury, involved an innocent victim of poisoning and a corrupt favorite. In 1626 a physician named George Eglisham, who had been a friend and servant of the Hamilton family, published a pamphlet called The Fore-runner of Revenge. It consisted of two letters written from Frankfurt to Charles I and to the Houses of Parliament, accusing the Duke of Buckingham of having murdered the Marquis of Hamilton, who died in 1625. Eglisham noted the parallel between this episode and the Overbury affair, insisting that he could produce more evidence against Buckingham than there had been against Somerset before his case came to trial. He added, for good measure, the suggestion that the favorite had murdered James as well. Buckingham was impeached in 1628 but Charles I dissolved Parliament before the case could come to trial. The effect of the pamphlet was long-lasting; Wotton says that it helped to motivate Felton's murder of the Duke two years later.[2] And it was possible to carry suspicion farther still: Wilson implies that Charles I's dissolution of Parliament showed his indifference as to whether or not his father had been murdered.[3] Like the other scandalous stories this one was republished after the outbreak of the Civil War; it appeared in both 1642 and 1648, with a further accusation: that Eglisham himself had been murdered abroad, by agents of the Duke. Sir Edward Peyton adds the Earl of Southampton and his son to Buckingham's list of victims.[4]

For the subplot of Lennox and the Countess of Hertford, Osborne probably relied exclusively on one source, Wilson's History of Great Britain. This tells the strange history of the three marriages of the 'other' Frances Howard, the rejected lover who killed himself for grief, and Lennox's visits to her in disguise during her marriage to Hertford.

---

1. Truth Brought to Light and Discovered by Time (partly based on a pamphlet of 1643 called The Five Years of King James); A True and Historical Relation of the Poysoning of Sir Thomas Overbury.
2. Reliquiae Wottonianae, p.114.
3. History of Great Britain, p.287.
4. Divine Catastrophe of the House of Stuarts, pp.360-62.

The one detail for which I have found no source is the reference to Hertford's gravel pits and his daily exercise of digging in them. Perhaps Osborne was writing from personal knowledge. That Hertford took an interest in gardens is clear from the famous Elvetham entertainment of 1591, for which he constructed an artificial lake in the shape of a crescent moon in honor of Elizabeth I. But his achievements in Wiltshire--whatever they were--have been overshadowed by those of his neighbor, the Earl of Pembroke, at Wilton.[1]

Though many Commonwealth historians complain of the favoring of Popery under James and Charles, the scenes between Northampton and 'Signor Con' are entirely Osborne's invention. They could hardly be otherwise, since Con did not become papal agent until 1636. Peyton mentions him, and accuses Charles I of being a secret papist.[2] A tract of 1643, The Pope's Nuntios, or the Negotiations of Signor Panzani, Seignor Con, &c., may be the source not only of the name, but also of the political analysis in these scenes. A sinister Jesuit appears in part one of the pamphlet play Crafty Cromwell (1648), and a number of pamphlets, both royalist and parliamentarian, purported to show that a vast Catholic/Spanish spy network had been responsible for every disaster of the century.[3] Osborne's other works tend to suggest that the Catholic threat has been grossly exaggerated and that a Catholic England would not even be greatly to the Pope's advantage--a point on which Northampton and Con also agree.[4] Northampton's villainy consists not in his secret Catholicism but in his absence of any real religious conviction (a fact which he admits at the end of III, ii).

In his treatment of James I, on the other hand, Osborne sticks very close to the views of contemporary historians, which presumably are a faithful echo of the gossip of the early decades of the century. His central argument--that James was the chief cause of the Civil War--is one with which many later historians would agree. Few, however, would accept the other accusations against him:

1. Before he came to the throne, James had contemplated murdering Elizabeth I

---

1. See Roy Strong, The Renaissance Garden of England (London, 1979), pp.125-6.
2. Divine Catastrophe of the House of Stuarts, pp.376-81.
3. Eg., Mysteries of State Carried on by the Spanish Faction in England. (1651) and The Plots of Jesuits (1653).
4. Cf. Memoirs of King James, para.14.

Introduction   xxix

>   and had perhaps disposed of some of
>   his own children.
>   2. Prince Henry's death in 1612 was
>   the result of poison, administered
>   with James's approval.
>   3. James used the Overbury scandal as
>   an excuse to rid himself of Somerset,
>   having already fallen under the in-
>   fluence of Villiers; his apparent
>   kindness to his former favorite was
>   nothing but hypocrisy.

It is the second and third of these that are most insisted on in the play, and they represent the views not only of Osborne, but of Weldon and Wilson. He may not have read Peyton's book; at any rate, he passed up the opportunity to repeat several of its juicy pieces of information: Prince Henry was not really James's son; Queen Anne shut him up all night with a beautiful girl to make sure he learned about sex; she was pregnant at the time of her death, and her doctor was murdered to prevent him from revealing the fact.[1] Nor does he seem to accept the suggestion of <u>A Cat May Look Upon a King</u>, that James let Prince Charles and Buckingham go to Spain in 1623 in the hope that he would thus be rid of them both.[2]

A number of writers use the phrase 'king-craft' and attribute it to James himself. Weldon gives an account of this 'craft' in action, which probably inspired Osborne's portrayal of James in the scenes with Villiers and Somerset in Act V:

>   The Earle of Somerset never parted from
>   him with more seeming affection than at
>   this time, when he knew Somerset should
>   never see him more; and had you seen
>   that seeming affection, (as the author
>   himself did,) you would rather have be-
>   lieved he was in his rising than setting.
>   The earle, when he kissed his hand, the
>   king hung about his neck, slabbering his
>   cheeks, saying, "For Gods sake, when
>   shall I see thee again?..."

---

1. <u>Divine Catastrophe of the House of Stuarts</u>, pp.344-8.
2. p.69.

But, Weldon goes on,

> The earl was not in his coach when
> the king used these very words, (in
> the hearing of four servants, of
> whom one was Somerset's great creature,
> and of the Bed-Chamber, who reported it
> instantly to the author of this history,)
> "I shall never see his face more." 1.

It seems to me likely that the Biblical words which Osborne attributes to the jury which tried Mary Queen of Scots-- "Her blood be upon us" (p. 18)-- are based on Weldon's claim that James himself called down a curse on the Stuarts.

Weldon, like Osborne, tends to stress the occasions on which he was a witness of episodes in his history. Yet most of these historians, despite the opportunities which they undoubtedly had for direct observation of great men, sound curiously unconvincing. To some extent, this may be the result of the moralizing yet sensational tone which they adopt toward their material. They prize the striking anecdote above the accurate date. Osborne himself declares in his Preface to the Historical Memoirs that he is little bothered about 'the exact calculation of Time, which rightly weighed, is but the pedantick part of History'. He regards letters (collections like the Cabala, presumably) as 'the best and purest intelligence'.2 Indeed, the alternative title of these works, Traditional Memoirs, suggests that, for him, what was thought to be true mattered more than what actually happened; hence, his frequent citation in the Memoirs of lampoons and epigrams. Thus, his claim to be an eye-witness of events has to be seen in the light of the preface already quoted:

> *It is ordinarily affirmed,* I have seen this
> or that, *when the most of it hath arrived
> at us from* Report. *And in this sense, I
> may be said to have seen* these, *and a number
> more, which out of respect to* others Fame,
> *or mine owne* Safety, *I wilfully omit. But
> lest this* Confession *might seem to cast a*

---

1. Court and Character of James I, pp.411-12.
2. Memoirs of King James, para.45.

Introduction

> *vail of prejudice over the face of that
> Truth I here expose to the curious eyes
> of this Age, as nakedly as Modesty will
> give a toleration for, I shall say in be-
> half of Tradition, that all Books are her
> Tenements, and contain little of History,
> whatever they may do of Invention, but
> what they hold from Manner of some Report
> or other.*

In the context of this attitude to history, The True Tragi-comedy does not seem wildly inaccurate. Most of the events of the play can be loosely fitted into the first nine months of 1613, but Osborne insists in his prologue on the poetic license to tamper with chronology and allow 'those to speak, that lived not in the year'--for instance, Stone the Fool, who was dead by 1606, and Simon Forman, who died in 1611. Apart from the scenes with Signor Con, already mentioned, the greatest liberties are taken at the beginning and end of the play. Even if the first three scenes are thought of as a sort of prologue, taking place some time before Salisbury's death in 1612, it is difficult to reconcile the reference to Prince Henry in the past tense in Scene iv with the fact that it is supposed to take place on the morning after Essex's wedding night. Chronology is stretched still further at the end. James promises that Lennox's wedding shall be the next after Somerset's, whereas there was an eight year gap between the two.

About minor details, Osborne is frequently, and under-standably, wrong. Few readers of the play will be disturbed to learn that Carr, who is called Somerset throughout, did not acquire his earldom until after the divorce, or that the references to 'my lady Wallingford' and 'Lord Carlisle' are equally anachronistic.

These inaccuracies are different from the deliberate and blatant use of hindsight which pervades the entire play. Occasionally this can be called dramatic irony, as in Helwys' vow, 'Let the Tower be the prospect of my ruin', if he fails to treat his prisoner well. More often, it takes the form of prophecy--not serious prophecy, like Cranmer's speech at the end of Henry VIII, but something more like the Fool's doggerel in Lear, followed by 'This prophecy Merlin shall make, for I live before his time'. Osborne obviously did not have much sympathy with such Civil War prophets as Booker and Lilly, or their less famous acquaintance John Heydon who had attacked Advice to a Son, and he shows Forman to be a charlatan who is able to identify Lady Frances only because he has already been eavesdropping on her conversation. But the references to the supposed statements of Lapland witches, wizards, conjurors, or anonymous sources who have 'foretold' events, allow Osborne both to have his historical irony and to make fun of it at the same time.

The fact that Osborne views the events of 1613 from a post-1649 perspective explains many aspects of his work. Of the characters who appear in the play, only one (Sir Benjamin Rudyerd) might still have been alive at the time of writing. Somerset, who died in obscurity in 1645, is the only major character who lived to see the Civil War. But when one looks at the large number of characters who are named, though they do not appear, it is clear that Osborne has been thinking primarily of those who took the side of Parliament in the War. These include Philip Earl of Montgomery, who succeeded his brother as Earl of Pembroke; the Earl of Essex, who became commander of the Parliamentary forces; William Cecil, the second Earl of Salisbury; Algernon Percy, son to the imprisoned Earl of Northumberland; such civil servants as John Packer and Sir William Uvedale, both of whom had been followers of Somerset; and indeed the Duke of Bedford, who had married the only child of the Somerset marriage. Rudyerd himself was a distinguished supporter of the Parliamentary cause, and it is noticeable that he is one of the few characters with whom Osborne seems to have any sympathy. Their political views were probably similar: Rudyerd was essentially a moderating voice in the opposition to the king, was in favor of an accommodation with him in 1648, and withdrew from political life after this date.

The Play as Tragicomedy

In Harbage and Schoenbaum's _Annals of English Drama_, the _True Tragicomedy_ is classified as a 'thesis play'. The 'thesis', I think, can be found in the opening paragraph of Osborne's _Memoirs of King James_:

> The _misfortunes_ of _Charles Stuart_,[1] Son to _King James_, with the uncouth, dismall and unexpressible calamities that happened thereupon, appear yet so great a Sacrifice in the Opinions of all interested by losse, or suborned by that natural propensity inherent in the most to expunge or palliate the Lapses of unhappy Princes (whose indulgence is not seldom so diffusive as to expiate for the faults of those standing in a far remoter relation than that of a Father)

1. Altered to 'King Charles' in post-1660 editions.

Introduction

> that they have hitherto stopped my
> Pen from making any farther progresse
> this way; Till, led on by a zeale to
> truth, and illuminated from the brighter
> Judgments of others, I found not only
> the imprudent *Commissions,* but volun-
> tary *Omissions* of *King James* so much
> instrumentall in the promotion of our
> present evills, as it may justly be
> said, He, like *Adam,* by bringing the
> Crown into so great a Necessity through
> a profuse prodigality, became the
> originall of his Son's fall: who was
> in a manner compel'd to stretch out his
> hands towards such gatherings and *Taxes,*
> as are contrary to Law: by which he
> fell from the *Paradise* of a Prince, to
> wit, The *hearts* of His People.

The final image is extremely forced: both James and Charles are Adam (with perhaps a hint that James might even be seen as the serpent); the forbidden fruit is Ship Money and the Forced Loan; and Paradise means the love of one's subjects. Yet it is highly characteristic of the tendency of writers in the 1650s to regard themselves as living in a fallen world, just as those of the 1630s had seen themselves as miraculously spared from (or shamefully escaping from) the wars which since 1619 had ravaged the world outside their 'paradise'. Thus, Marvell could apostrophize England as 'the garden of the world e'erwhile', and ask,

> What luckless apple did we taste,
> To make us mortal, and thee waste?

It will be noticed that none of these images of the Fall includes a counterpart to Eve. Osborne's treatment of the Essex divorce does not specifically identify Frances Howard with this role, but it is strikingly misogynistic. By not allowing Essex to appear, Osborne keeps attention focussed entirely on the husband's sexual inadequacy rather than his personality and emphasizes the absence, in Frances, of any-thing apart from appetite. At her first entrance, she de-clares, 'you know I am no virgin', and we are reminded that Prince Henry was one of many earlier lovers. In some ver-sions of the story, Frances and Carr had been lovers even be-fore Essex's return to claim his bride; here, we see Somer-set delicately offering his help to a woman who pretends to be too innocent to understand her husband's inadequacy, yet has really fallen in love with Somerset through Mrs.Turner's

account of his sexual prowess. It is equally in keeping
with this misogynistic treatment that the instigator of the
adultery should be Mrs. Turner and not, as in some versions,
Northampton or his servant Copinger.[1] The other women of
the play (apart from the anonymous virgin, who is compared
to Eve before she 'turned costard-monger to the serpent')
are almost as sexually insatiable as Frances. Both the
Countess of Hertford and her maid are called daughters of
Eve, and we are reminded of the man who killed himself for
love of the Countess. Naturally, against this background of
rapacious and destructive women, Somerset himself seems more
a victim than a agent. The conclusion of Osborne's Character of him-- 'His folly was in suffering his reason to be
stifled by the vapors of lust'--suggests that he saw the fall
of the favorite as a repetition of the archetypal fall of man.

In the Roos case of 1619, according to Chamberlain,
James I 'spoke long and excellently to every point, comparing this to the first judgement, Sir Thomas Lake to Adam, his
Lady to Eve, and the Lady Rosse to the serpent.'[2] It is
clear, of course, who represents God in this situation.
Within Osborne's play, everyone from the king on down seems
to play God to his immediate subordinates. Both Salisbury
and Somerset see James as their 'Maker',[3] and Osborne in his
Character of Somerset describes Winwood as having fallen
'from his Maker (Somerset)...almost in as short time as the
Rabbins assign to Adam in Paradise' (p.6).

These images of the Fall can best be understood in relation to the tragicomic design. One of the oddest things
about Osborne's handling of the story is the way in which he
consistently bypasses its numerous opportunities for death
scenes. Forman, Salisbury, and Overbury himself, all disappear from the action without any indication of what happens to them. By reading between the lines, we can deduce
Prince Henry's death between I,i, where he is said to be
ill, and I, iv, where his name is followed by 'God rest his
soul!' Similarly, the death of Salisbury can be guessed from

---

1. Eg., in Weldon, Court and Character of King James, p.389;
   Wilson describes Northampton persuading James to support
   the divorce (History, p.68).
2. Chamberlain, Letters, ed. N. McLure, 2 Vols. (Philadelphia, 1939), II, p.214.
3. TT, I,ii,49; V,iii,21.

the fact that Northampton in III, iii, is shown to covet the now vacant post of Treasurer. Osborne does not apply his usual hindsight to point out the irony of this ambition, in view of the fact that Northampton himself was to die in June 1614. Nor does he choose to end his story with either the death of Overbury or the fall of Somerset and Frances, which would have pointed a moral of sorts. There are few plays which end with villainy so completely triumphant.

So the play as we see it is a comedy, ending in traditional comic fashion with two marriages. But James's final couplet reminds us that this comedy is embedded in a larger story: Somerset's

> joys here end, or our diviners lie
> That say the next will prove a tragedy.

The tragedy in question is not only that of Somerset, but that of the house of Stuart. The linking of main plot and subplot, though chronologically forced, is thematically right: both Somerset and Lennox are Scottish favorites of the King, both commit adultery with Frances Howard (representative of a corrupt English family), and both are rewarded for their immorality by an immoral ruler. James begins and ends the play, because it is with him that responsibility for the action ultimately rests. The confusion in Osborne's Fall of Man imagery is hardly surprising: what he wishes to say, I think, is that James is both God and Satan, creator and tempter--and his son, of course, will have to play the role of Christ, or Charles the Martyr.

The interest of *The True Tragicomedy*, then, lies neither in its value as a play nor in its claim to be an eye-witness account of history: such new information as it contains is of the gossipy sort likely to be of interest only to historians of sexual mores. It belongs, rather, to the genre of Osborne's other historical works, and other histories written in the 1650s. Robert Ashton sums them up very well: 'they present a view of the king which came to be held by many of his subjects, and perhaps by an increasing number of them, as his reign drew on to its close. However unreliable and unfair these accounts may be, they are material which no historian can afford to neglect.[1]

---

1. *James I by His Contemporaries* (London, 1969), pp.xx-xxi. The only historian to draw on *The True Tragicomedy*, so far as I know, is G.P.V. Akrigg, *Jacobean Pageant* (London 1962).

This Edition

Since even Osborne himself could hardly have wished to publish MS 25348 in its present state, I have followed the example of his seventeenth century editors in breaking up some of his longest sentences, introducing paragraphing, standardizing his spelling and punctuation, and correcting what seemed to be straightforward errors. To retain seventeenth-century spelling seemed pointless in the circumstances, so this is a modernized text. Where there seemed any possibility that the MS might bear another interpretation than mine, I have given the original spelling or wording in a footnote. The distinction between correction and emendation is, of course, not always easy to draw, but I hope that the resulting text will be adequate to most scholarly purposes.

Both the characters and the play are a riot of topical allusions. To avoid making the pages bottom-heavy, I have explained these in the Biographical Dictionary wherever possible. I have also tried to avoid excessive paraphrasing of Osborne's numerous stylistic obscurities, hoping that the reader will get used to them in time. Mid-seventeenth-century prose is often contorted, and mid-seventeenth-century blank verse often lacks a sense of form. A useful context for Osborne's style is provided by some of the hilarious examples quoted in Alfred Harbage's Cavalier Drama.[1]

The author's own notes, originally in the margin of the MS, appear here as footnotes, enclosed in quotation marks and followed by '(O)'. A dash in the text indicates an omission on Osborne's part; he himself sometimes uses a dash and sometimes a blank. Some of his omissions are due to lapses of memory, some to laziness, and some, apparently, to a desire to tease, but I have not found any consistency in his manner of indicating them.

His own stage-directions and act and scene numbering have been retained, except in one place (III,i) where he has clearly got something wrong. I have also used his speech prefixes, even though this means that the Countess of Suffolk is referred to throughout as 'Old Kate'. Stage directions or words supplied by me are in square brackets.

---

1. See, esp., pp.36-39, and 222-24.

Introduction   xxxvii

    I should like to express my gratitude for help and advice received from the staffs of the Huntington Library, San Marino, California, and the British Library (especially Mr. Hilton Kelliher of the Department of Manuscripts). Dr. John Pitcher of St. John's College, Oxford, who first suggested the desirability of editing this manuscript, shared the task of transcription with me and gave me the benefit of his extensive knowledge of the Jacobean court. No one but myself, however, is responsible for any errors in the introduction, notes, or biographical dictionary.

                                         Lois Potter
                                         University of Leicester

BIBLIOGRAPHICAL NOTE

While there are a great many early editions of Osborne's works, there is no standard one: see Francis F. Madan, 'Some Notes on the Bibliography of Francis Osborne', Oxford Bibliographical Society Publications, N.S. IV(1950), pp.55-60. Advice to a Son is available in the editions of E.A. Parry (1896) and Louis B. Wright (1962); the Historical Memoirs can be found in Vol. I of Walter Scott, ed., Secret History of the Court of James the First, 2 Vols. (Edinburgh, 1811). The other works are still unedited. For the sake of uniformity, I have quoted from the first edition throughout, giving references to chapters, subsections, paragraphs, etc., rather than pages.

Other works frequently cited are:

Chamberlain: John Chamberlain, Letters, ed. N. McLure, 2 Vols. (Philadelphia, 1939).
Fuller: Thomas Fuller, Worthies of England (1662)
Gardiner: S.R. Gardiner, History of England from the Accession of James I to the Outbreak of the Civil War 1603-1642, 10 Vols. (1883-84), Vol. II.
Weldon: Anthony Weldon, Court and Character of King James (1650).
Wilson: Arthur Wilson, History of Great Britain, being the Life and Reign of King James the First (1653).

A page of the manuscript of *The True Tragicomedy*

Robert Devereux, Third Earl of Essex

Edward Seymour, Earl of Hertford

Frances Howard, Countess of Hertford

Lodovick Stuart, Duke of Lennox

Henry Howard, Earl of Northampton

James VI and I

Robert Cecil, Earl of Salisbury

George Villiers, Duke of Buckingham

Simon Forman

Sir Thomas Overbury

Anne Turner

Sir Gervase Helwys, Lieutenant of the Tower

THE
TRUE TRAGI-COMEDY
FORMERLY ACTED AT COURT
AND NEWLY REVIVED BY AN
EYE-WITNESS
BEFORE WHICH ARE DRAWN
THE
LIVELY PICTURES
OR CHARACTERS
OF THE
MOST CONSIDERABLE PERSONS
REPRESENTED

TO THE READER

concerning the following characters or pictures

After the play was finished, I undertook these pictures, that may not impossibly outlast their marble that own them (the soldier pretending the houses of the dead as well as the living to lie inclusive in his bill of plunder).[1] I thought, with my fellow poets, to have only touched upon the humors of the most considerable persons represented, but my pen is become so much my mistress as I can neither stop her career nor force her on where she likes not the way. Therefore I desire pardon for the length no less than the rudeness of the draughts, which, besides the insufficiency of the workman's infirmities, have had so many years to deface them in my memory as they cannot choose but be subject to more mistakes than I am able to mend, which could not have happened had they been committed out of malice or respect.[2] However such as they are may be buried in their use who desire to understand the comedy, or laid, as a number of such spurious births are, at the door of oblivion. And, since I have so far exceeded my design, I may (as a builder that endeavors the content of passengers)[3] have advanced likely some stories higher, and set out more lights,[4] than was at first intended[5] or do indeed justly fall under the primitive model.

---

1. A reference both to the commonplace claim that literature will outlast monuments of bronze or marble, and to the desecration of churches and their contents during the Civil War.
2. <u>respect</u>: excessive deference.
3. <u>passengers</u>: passers-by.
4. <u>lights</u>: windows.
5. <u>intended</u>: 'intend' in MS.

If these condemn me which are but scribblers themselves, I appeal from their judgements, as incompetent, if they be, for partial, and inconsiderate[1] to pierce their credit through the sides of mine, before they know their own fate: many authors being thought worthy to be saved by us which the forefathers damned to the pit of Hell. I amongst others hissed Sejanus off the stage, yet after sat it out, not only patiently but with content and admiration. Everyone owns not judgement, and such as do, carry it not always about them, thinking themselves unconcerned till they hear a book praised or dispraised; and then, for their own honor rather than truth's, they will maintain the contrary to what was said, be it good or bad. So as, if the sense of idleness were not more pricking and tedious, a man would, by lying still, rather bear the weight[2] of forgetfulness than leave anything to bring his name under that of the printer, who, like the jailor, doth not only take him with such faults as he hath committed but renders his work,[3] before it goes out of his hand, sevenfold more the child of ignorance than the author left it. And, though it be our unhappy fate to hear not seldom our wounded reputations, like the body of Hector, drawn about the streets after our death, yet, in hope of a rescue by some friends, I have altered a late resolution took to cut out and burn some quires, if not most of what I had writ, to prevent the former misfortune,[4] which mercenary people expose orphan papers to.

It is natural with mortals to covet a place in the chariot of Fame, though known to alter her carriage at every stage, taking in fresh opinion and throwing out the old; having no constant passengers[5] but Reason, which still keeps her seat and continues the journey without wagging, though unmannerly crowded and vexed by the tedious and canting discourses of scholars, as such poor innocent women whose lot falls out to pass in a University crack.[6] Yet upon this frail desire of immortality all monuments are built, from the most stately colleges to the low and phlegmatic grave-stones whose inscriptions are washed out with the spittle and feet of the living; and tedious marriage contracted out of a no more serious

---

1. inconsiderate: imprudent.
2. weight: 'wait' in MS. O. may intend both meanings.
3. work: 'worth' in MS.
4. the former misfortune: posthumous publication.
5. passengers: 'paingors' in MS.
6. crack: noise.

To the Reader

account than to purchase an heir, that may continue their line, and transmit their image and likeness to eternity. Not so durable many times as an impress upon wax, or the walks raised by the Earl of Hertford, which do now celebrate his memory as much as they did once depair[1] it, it appearing a ridiculous sight in the eyes of our sprucer judgements for a lord to drive a wheelbarrow. Nor may it better become me in the like apprehensions to write a play, much less own it, with all the levities and imperfections it may be thought guilty of. Which I do with the greater confidence because I have no better way to take my imagination off from poring upon my misfortunes than by letting it run a wool-gathering, nor can I worthily be capable of blame to desire the preservation of what I have picked up. It not being impossible but posterity may make something of it, or at least patch up the wants hereafter to be found perhaps in the more perfect labor of other men; since the most we hear of Henry II, Lewis XI, Pope Alexander VI, etc., are gleaned out of letters, lawyers' records, and other waste papers such as mine. But however this proves, I am naturally well pleased for the time, like the father of Seneca's fool, who might possibly take as much delight in his production as he that begat the Stoic himself.

This I am sure I have learned by the way, that the best wits for the most part are not so faithful to the actions and persons they character as your downright narrators that hear nothing to bias them: a fine sentence, observation, or a neat rencontre being such rubs as the other are not able to pass without tugging.[2] I hope I am no more guilty of this fault than concerned in the occasion that creates it: my pen in all her paces[3] being apter to start at a lie, though probable and neat, than to refuse the way of truth, though pestered with never so many contrary opinions. Yet as a horse doth pass without notice many greater _____ than at other times he blancheth at, so may I. Which being without malice or design, will, I hope, with the more ease be pardoned, especially

---

1. depair: impair.
2. tugging: struggling. 'touging' in MS; perhaps 'touching'? 'Rubs' and 'bias' are metaphors from bowling. A bowl was weighted to give it a bias, a term which also applied to the angle at which it was thrown. Rubs were obstacles in the course.
3. paces: 'pases' in MS.

to him that was never owner of their reciprocal, if not
dear-bought obligations. For any affections to a cause
or person (a felon[1] incident to the fingers of historians, and doth not seldom rob posterity of truth) I have
done what I can to palliate it. But it's so inveterate
and natural as I despair of a perfect cure. Yet had we
as certain records of the beginning of this line[2] as
may be found among my Memoirs concerning the concluding
of it (if God in his mercy to England do not knit it
again),[3] they would be highly esteemed. All mine wants
is age, old stories being for rareness new, and new (by
reason of a contemporary apprehension) stale. Therefore, if these can but resist the injuries of time till
age hath given them maturity, it is possible they may
crowd in amongst the rest till a more happy ignorance
shall have swallowed them up with all books else: not
thought by me any promoters of felicity in this world,
or advancers of the belief of that to come.

The Earl of Somerset

He was of a fair complexion, equally sharing the beauty
of both sexes (therefore thought by his recommenders
the fittest subject for the humour of King James).
Holding a mediocrity in his stature as he was, at his
reception, imagined to own in his judgement - much refined by an opportunity took from leisure he attained
by a broken leg, in which he so happily improved his
pen that I have heard him numbered among the first who
did not only frizzle and powder hair, but letters of
state, no less to the trouble of barbers than public
ministers. Which went so against the grain of Sir Ralph
Winwood's head, uncapable of either, that he fell from
his maker (Somerset), and listened to the counsel of
his enemies, almost in as short a time as the Rabbins
assign to Adam in Paradise.[4] Though during the favor-

---

1. <u>felon</u>:felony; or perhaps 'failing'?
2. <u>this line</u>: the Stuarts.
3. If O. actually left an account of the reign of Charles I, it has disappeared.
4. The length of Adam's stay in Paradise, in Rabbinical traditions, varied from five and a half hours to seven years. See C.A. Patrides, <u>Milton and the Christian Tradition</u> (Oxford, 1966), p.108, n.1.

The Earl of Somerset

able aspect upon their planet many things succeeded unluckily to the nation, yet the most of them happened by the mediation of others, without his conjunction. Who never, like his successor,[1] monopolised favor, but connived at the suits of his fellow-courtiers, which made greater of his own pass with the less bruit. He gave the later ear to his particular ambition, out of hopes to preserve the ancient nobility from overwhelming and to stop the wandorcers[2] of honor [which] the covetousness of his countrymen, no less than the improvidence of his master, had set open to all able to number money or friends. And if the Baronets crawled up in his time,[3] I may safely say it was out of their Treasurer's[4] corruption and not his. Who had few friends or kindred distinguishable from others by the mark of his favor: the cause his fall was with no greater shout of the people, though to the ever-odious name of Minion his birth had unhappily added that of a Scot.

He had no natural title to the quarrels Queen Anne, Prince Henry, William Earl of Pembroke, etc., contracted with him, which upon serious examination will be found rather to be concubinary[5] to his master's jealousies and fears than a legitimate issue of any humor resident in him - that participated more of the sheep whose fleece he carried than the lion. Which yet he acted so well in the Tower that he changed the King's warrant for his execution and his Lady's into a gracious pardon. And for a farther demonstration of the goodness of his nature, he offered to submit himself in all humility to the prince,[6] which the King reproved him for, saying openly that his[7] choice of

---

1. his successor: Buckingham.
2. wandorcers: perhaps a conflation of 'windows' and 'doors'.
3. the Baronets crawled up in his time: the title of Baronet was created in 1611 as a money-making device (it cost about £1000).
4. their Treasurer: the Earl of Salisbury and his successor, the Earl of Suffolk.
5. concubinary: relating to the children of concubines, hence, illegitimate.
6. the prince: Prince Charles (Henry had died in 1612).
7. his: the King's (ie., James had more faith in his favorites than in his wife's children, who might or might not be his own).

men was with more deliberation than of his wives. Nor did
he ever comply with that design the King was reported to
have brought in his bosom out of Scotland, till Prince [1]
Henry had discovered an irreparable intention to revenge.
His happy arrival before the tree was quite shaken, which[2]
the sweetness of Queen Elizabeth's reign had _____[3]
with all things desirable to a people, made the vast sum
be found about him at his fall, the more easy to be
gathered without any notice of a Parliament which he owed
rather to his own moderation than the favor of the King
(who was too wary to interpose) or mediation of friends,
of which he numbered fewer than any that ever filled a
place of a far less magnitude. Neither did this[4] grow
from want of candor, but to spare the common wealth, know-
ing one accusation stains more than the fame of forty en-
comiums can rinse off.

Concerning the poisoning of Overbury, the general
opinion of that time did acquit him of all knowledge till
after the fact, yet if posterity measure his fault by the
greatness of the Judge Coke's hyperbolical and ridiculous
criminations, they may lay more to his charge than possibly he deserved; his folly was in suffering his reason
to be stifled by the vapors of lust.

The Lady Frances

Was a right spark of that fair diamond, the Lady Katherine
Audley,[5] Countess of Suffolk, who was of so invincible a
rock, as her lustre did not only exceed her eldest, but
lasted to be contemporary with this her youngest daughter.
Nor could her ruin, with the suppression of her family,
prevail farther than to shadow her face with gravity, no
less majestical than her youth was lovely.

---

1. A reference to the belief that the King and his favorite
   connived at the murder of Prince Henry (see Introduction,
   p.xxx.
2. which: 'with' in MS.
3. Blank in MS (probably 'laden'?).
4. this: Somerset's secret hoarding of wealth.
5. Audley: Osborne is mistaken. Audley was the family name of
   her husband's mother, after whom the great Suffolk house of
   Audley End was named. The Countess was born Lady
   Katherine Knyvet or Knevet.

The Lady Frances

Not to register the huge devastation the beauty of the
Countess of Essex caused in the hopes, hearts, estates
and understandings of subjects, it grew to be a common
report that Prince Henry was so captivated by her eyes,
which then found no matches but themselves, that the house
of Suffolk took the boldness to own him for their prisoner
of love, and not likely to be changed. But, whether ran-
somed by the activity of his own judgement, the graver advice of others, or the freedom she might too soon allow
him, he gave her over in the face of all their expecta-
tions before her father had the leisure to object the
soliciting of a married lady for a fault, or the world
to calculate the disproportion of their births and folly
of such an attempt (her husband being son of the people's
darling,[1] and all the hatchet had left them to bestow
their insignificant clamors upon: therefore unlikely[2]
to own any imperfections in him, especially one so ridiculous and unsuitable to the complexion of his father:
else the novelty of her disaster would rather have
whetted than rebated the desire in men of honor to redeem her).

Amongst things of like weight, which the rabble
talked[3] up to bespatter her fame, was the invention of
yellow starch, the proper foil to set off beauty, and
palliate ugliness, for which lies ready as plain a defence as our ancestors could make for the wearing of
blue. If her enemies find room to judge her no virgin,
because Mrs Shirley was searched in her stead,[4] I desire
them to consider the diligence used before she could be
found, or any else able to stand the taste[5] of such a
trial: therefore, if women, they must hold their peace
or predicate[6] their own shame.

How though[7] her life and person cannot in all points
be justified against the censure of those pass not only
wisdom but religion in magnifying the sins of others,
and mincing[8] their own, I hope her more innocent picture may be allowed still to adorn the cabinet of our

---

1. the people's darling: Queen Elizabeth's favorite, beheaded
   in 1601.
2. unlikely: refers to 'the people'.
3. talked: 'taked' in MS. Perhaps 'raked'?
4. See Introduction, p. xxi.
5. taste: 'tast' in MS; perhaps 'test'?
6. predicate: proclaim.
7. How though: although.
8. mincing: minimizing.

Princes, as it doth at this day that of the Great Mogul
to whom it being presented by Sir Thomas Roe did so far
advance his conversion as to confess, God was more immediately among the Christians than Mahometans, else they
could never produce such angelical shapes.[1]
   She lived after her enlargement long under the same
roof with Somerset, yet unconcerned as a wife, he looking upon her as the author of his fall - which without
doubt was long before decreed in the will of the King,
who was glad to embrace the occasion. Though the Italian
Divinity were true, that no sin below the girdle is mortal, yet an effect of it may be so, as experience did
manifest in this Lady, who died of a disease in those
parts. After the inspiration of a daughter (the Countess
of Bedford) with as much beauty and virtue as the mother
may be imagined to have had or wanted.

Sir Thomas Overbury

I cannot deny the general report so much credit but to believe that, though Overbury was of excellent parts, the
prodigiousness of his pride was far the greater miracle, a

---

1. O. is conflating two episodes from Roe's journal, part
   of which was published by Samuel Purchas in 1625. Lady
   Frances's portrait, along with that of her sister
   (called Lady Cranborne in TT), the King and Queen of
   England, and a number of others, was displayed at the
   court of the Great Mogul during the New Year's feast
   (2 March, 1615). Roe does not mention its presence the
   following year (12 March, 1616), probably because by
   then he had heard of the Somersets' trial for murder.
   But the picture which Roe presented (or rather, was
   forced to present) to the Mogul was that of an unknown
   woman whom he described as 'the image of one that I
   loved dearly and could never recover'. The Mogul 'confessed he never saw so much Art, so much Beauty; and
   conjured me to tell him truely, whether ever such a
   woman lived.' (Purchas His Pilgrims, ed. MacLehose,
   20 Vols, 1905-7: Vol IV, pp.331, 353-4, and 398).

The Earl of Northampton

copy of which may be found under his own hand in some of
his dispatches from the Tower, not exceeded in height by
many I have yet seen dated from the Throne. His contest[1]
was directed, by fortune or the presumption of his own
power, against persons of that eminency as he deserved
not the name of an almanac-maker that could not prognos-
ticate almost the very death he died: for had not the
males of the house of Suffolk (to whose vengeance his
ordinary enemies left him) been more phlegm than choler,
he had not perished by so fair a hand. It was ordinary
with him to take his lord's coach from the court gate and
leave him to seek, speaking still in the imperative upon
the least occasion of heat, so as had he lived under the
meridian of the court of France, he had begun and ended
his pomp the same day.[2] According to the humor of his
style, he was gracious to men of parts, as Sir Benjamin
Rudyerd, Sir H. Gu,[3] etc., with whose wits he clubbed for
those few things he printed; not that he wanted of his
own, but in detestation to be outgone. To conclude, his
sin was pride and fullness of a presumptuous learning that
left no room for advice and experience to do the good
offices they might. Which Mr. John Packer wanting, or
having them at better command, enjoyed the King's favor,
riches, and honor, with long life, the most, if not all,
which the other missed of.

The Earl of Northampton

Lay the most considerable part of his days, in relation to
his actions, under the cloud of his prince's displeasure,
or, what a noble nature brooks worse, her contempt and neglect. So as my first memory found him lodged over the
gate where now is Sutton's Hospital, in the Charterhouse;

---

1. <u>contest</u>: enmity.

2. Cf. O's remarks on Overbury in his essay, 'It is the condition of those in Power to be guided by Servants': 'he
   offered to rant at his [Somerset's] <u>Servants</u>, and did once
   beat the <u>Coach-man</u>, for putting his <u>Commands</u> under an in-
   feriour expostulation to his <u>Masters.</u>' (<u>Miscellany</u>,p.256).

3. <u>Sir H. Gu</u>: Sir Henry Goodyere?

and this unsuitable condition, to a mind in its own
apprehension capable of the highest employment, acquainted him with a subtle kind of stalking towards
all, though but in small and trivial things, as rendered what he did or said suspected of design. Which
scared King James from that confidence which is natural
for princes to have of them they raise and so left him
the opener yet for his enemies, that were the more because he had so few friends; it being unlikely any
should such as at least[1] they do not believe themselves
able to fathom. This[2] made it commonly reported that
the Earl of Northampton, no less than his brother of
Suffolk (looked upon for the honester man), were made
chaplains in the temples of honor to celebrate, by this
gratitude to their children that suffered with her,[3]
the memory of his Majesty's mother, which he seemed to
make sacred. (Nor was it unseasonable neither to prefer[4]
Cecil and divers Scots, though apparently sprinkled with
her blood, lest it might have been shown by whose warrant it was shed;[5] and, to keep this from remaining a
perpetual bridle to the Scotch line, the Earl of Salisbury was no sooner dead but his papers were searched:
not usually done in my time by entreaty, much less under
the severe countenance of a constraint - which could not

---

1. <u>at least</u>: 'lest' in MS; perhaps 'last'? The construction of this phrase is difficult; it probably means that a man as hard to fathom as Northampton was unlikely to have many friends.
2. <u>This</u>: Queen Elizabeth's enmity to the Howards.
3. <u>their children that suffered with her</u>: the children of those who died for their intrigues in the cause of Mary Queen of Scots, as did Thomas Howard, Duke of Norfolk, in 1572. He was the father of the Earl of Suffolk and the brother of the Earl of Northampton. (O. consistently forgets that Northampton was Suffolk's uncle, not his brother.)
4. <u>prefer</u>: favor.
5. A hint that James had given a written consent to his mother's execution, presumably in his secret correspondence with the Cecils.

but question the civility of the living or integrity of
the dead.)   Not to quit my first man, Northampton was
advanced rather because he had lain under the displeasure
of Queen Elizabeth than any delight King James took in
him.   5
     He was by education as well as descent a Romish
Catholic, and so far zealous as to give order to be
buried at Rome - a thing after endeavored but how it
succeeded I know not.   Yet, to keep himself capable
of honors and preferments at court (of which he was the   10
most lickerish[1] man living, else he had never erected so
high a discontent out of his brother's assumption into
the then fatal chair of Treasurer),[2] he dissembled the
contrary. He never married, perhaps the cause report
numbered him amongst those had taken Orders: to which[3]   15
must be added his love to Spain, for a peace with whose
king he was a great stickler, though in discourse he
cried up our English hierarchy above the temporally.[4]
Such as pretended to know him best thought him no farther
concerned in religion than it produced profit at home and 20
esteem from abroad: not being utterly out of hope of a
Cardinal's cap, a dignity he could not refrain commending,
sometimes to the prejudice of what he desired to conceal.
     His leisure had given him time to rake up so much
learning as rendered him no less tedious to the wise than 25
unintelligible to the ignorant, of the truth of which a
surfeit may be taken by any that shall read his Gunpowder
Treason, and Discourse of Duels,[5] as I have had many by

---

1. lickerish: greedy.
2. See Appendix. O. describes the post of Treasurer as fatal,
   because, as Fuller later explained, it was one 'which in
   that age was hard to keep. Insomuch, that one asking,what
   was good to preserve Life? was answered, Get to be Lord
   Treasurer of England, for they never do dye in their place,
   which indeed was true for four successions.' (Worthies of
   England, 1662, p.211).
3. to which: ie., causes.
4. temporally: temporality.
5. his Gunpowder treason and Discourse of Duels: his speech
   against Father Henry Garnet, executed in 1606 for supposed
   complicity in the Gunpowder Plot, was published in a somewhat altered form that year. In 1613 he drew up James I's
   edict against duelling, and may also have written a pamphlet called Duellio Foiled which appeared at the same
   time, though it is not now ascribed to him.

his speeches in the Star Chamber, where he corroded the
ears of his auditors no less than of the poor offenders
with his tart sentences, not hard to be bettered out of
the schoolboy's poesy; so as I heard his brother desire
him to be brief, which I am confident he looked upon as a
greater indignity to the company than himself. So easily
may a scholar be carried on by the confidence that others
hear with as much delight as he speaks.[1]

He was an incomparable master to any that had no other
means but out of his own estate to prefer servants,[2] of
which he kept many at board wages, being maimed in house-
keeping for want of a wife, whose place may be imagined
stood not quite empty (especially in his youth) by the
full ripe expressions he useth in some of his letters publicly read at the Earl of Somerset's arraignment. For
anything farther concerning this nobleman, I am mistaken if
it may not (in a great part) be found among my papers entitled my Memoirs.

The Lord Treasurer Cecil

He had the fortune to be the prudent son of a most incomparable wise father, who, though of different education
and extraction (the one being the issue of a poor ostler,
the other of [a] noble and potent courtier), they were observed in matters of government to steer one and the same
way; and if any advantage appeared in the magnificence
and splendour of their department, standers-by awarded it
rather to the father than the son. Which may help to resolve a query, whether the child of a prince and that of a
cobbler be distinguishable by future demeanor. His face
and hands had a beauty in them above ordinary, but from
his neck to the middle he declined into a kind of bossive
antic[3] work, being very crooked and low.

The time of his employment under Queen Elizabeth (the
best housewife of the people's treasure that was ever en-
trusted with the management of a sceptre), he complied

---

1. he speaks: 'they speak' in MS.
2. Ie., for someone in his financial position, he was a good master ('incomparable' is rather a contradiction here).
3. bossive: hunchbacked.
   antic: grotesque.

The Lord Treasurer Cecil

with equity and law; but after the worser luck of
England had made the Scotch King trump, he, like the
steward of [a] Sire that leaves an unworthy heir, wheeled
his care about towards himself and becomes as ready as
the rest to impropriate that [which] his father's wisdom
and his own had gotten, or at least preserved, for the
use of the state. Since he cannot be thought to have
loved Spain, with whom he had not only inherited a war
but continued it by his own advice, much less, in charity,
can I impute his desire of peace to the donative sent him
by that prince,[1] reported to be very considerable. The
buying and selling the secrets, honor, and safety of
England not being reckoned to him in the large bill of reproaches and prejudices writ on the people's hearts with
the Earl of Essex's blood, which no endeavor of his could
expunge his life, nor[2] any apology of friends discharge
him of at his grave. This makes me incline to their
opinions that impute the something dishonorable pardon
granted to that almost overrun traitor Tyrone,[3] and the
peace made with the panting and embossed Spaniard,[4] not
as slips in his fidelity or prudence but a result
yielded to an urgent necessity. Hoping, by keeping
things quiet without, to open the better all obstruc-
tions that might, by stopping the progress of the Scotch
line, entangle the nation in a war at home. The blessed
star that guided us having so far lost her activity as
she began about this time to hover over her tomb;[5]
therefore, so many titles being under numeration, and no
successor declared, he could not provide better against
civil commotion (the only thing dreadful to the wise
Council of that age) than by removing out of their sight
all things the people thought grievous.
    Time hath not yet quite robbed my memory of the huge
weight of indiscretion our Paul's-walking politicians[6]

---

1. Cecil, like many other courtiers, was in receipt of an annual pension from Spain.
2. nor: 'not' in MS.
3. Tyrone: Hugh O'Neill, Earl of Tyrone, was offered a pardon by Elizabeth, though she had died by the time he capitulated.
4. By the treaty of London, 1604.
5. Elizabeth I, like the Star of Bethlehem in reverse, is described as leading the way to her own tomb.
6. Cf. Introduction, pp. vi-vii.

(who were many, and of no despicable parts) loaded their elder brethren with[1] at Whitehall, especially when they saw James bury the Englishman's hopes in his partiality to the Scots. Coming short in performance of what the expectation of all (wearied with a feminine government) had engaged him to, which[2] he surpassed in nothing but riot and excess, the parents of oppression and fomenters of the people's discontent, not uneasy to be formed into such rational complaints: that, if by the law a man born in Scotland out of an ambassador's house was rendered incapable to inherit a cottage in England before his nature was purified by an act of Parliament, much less could an alien's title be legitimate in relation to the Crown between which and his ancestors there had been such irreconcilable feuds as no marriage, obligation or oath was ever yet able to palliate upon the least apprehension of an advantage; or, if thought to dissemble, by the vastness of their hopes it might easily have been presaged that such multitudes would crowd into the bowels of the nation, under pretence of sore[3] to their own King, as might occasion more mischief than the Border had yet peace from their swords.

Nor could his descent from the eldest sister[4] be admitted for so canonical a place, since her brother's will, made by the consent of the three estates, had omitted that family; done without question out of a serious apprehension of what we now lie under. And though the deed itself may have been embezzled and taken off the file by Leicester and out of hope to marry the Queen, yet the Cursitor that enrolled it, and many that have seen it, were that day ready to be produced.[5] But if no chain was thought strong

---

1. with: 'which' in MS. Ie., with hindsight, the political gossips blamed those councillors who had given their consent to James I's accession.
2. which: refers to 'expectation', perhaps also to Queen Elizabeth.
3. sore: so in MS. Perhaps means 'harm'.
4. the eldest sister: Margaret Tudor, sister of Henry VIII, and Queen of James IV of Scotland.
5. Cf. Memoirs of Queen Elizabeth: 'Nor was an inquisition after the Will of Henry the 8th omitted, which a Cursitor did about that time justify he had inrolled, though then not to be found, having before been taken off the File by some as small friends to the Scottish title as any other but their own' (para.24). A Cursitor was a clerk of the Court of Chancery.

enough to yoke us save one made of a link of Henry VII, why should not our countrymen - Hertford, Huntington, De la Pole - be preferred? Who could not be imagined to have owned so many poor kindred as this man did indigent nobles and commons. To pretend a possibility of succeeding by force were to proclaim a stupid ignorance in the juncture of those times, the name of a Scot being so odious then to a subject (nor is it much better read yet) that he who could but read the ballad of Chevy Chase might have in a few hours raised a regiment.
    Therefore, to speak English, we had little compulsion but what our own follies and fears created among us. For France, the only confidence of Scotland, was then shaken like a broken reed between the winds of two incompatible opinions, and that King[1] so shallow-rooted in his subjects' affections, as, if he could forget the money and assistance sent him from hence, to believe the favours done his enemies by the Catholic King,[2] his own interest would have withheld him from doing much, since this conjunction was likely in the future to occasion more jealousies than security to that nation, especially if under a belligerous prince,[3] which Henry, the heir of that family, was ever reported to be. The Spaniard begged our favor, or, if he should venture to cast in that line Parsons the Jesuit had twisted for him, he had nothing to bait it with, being himself poor and most of the English papists either wrought by reason or interest out of that creed. At the worst, the apparition of an English navy on the Indian straits would have restrained any further attempt, the baseness of the Irish having already betrayed him out of all confidence there. The Dutch government was too young to have her eyes open towards any interest but her own and ours that bred her so that, if London had then converted her Mayor into a Consul, and her aldermen into a Senate, the United Province would rather have assisted, in hopes to have drowned the report of their defection in this greater of ours.

---

1. <u>that king</u>: Henry IV.
2. <u>the Catholic King</u>: the King of Spain.
3. <u>belligerous</u>: belligerent, in the original Latin sense of 'making war'.

Nor is it probable the King of Scots had ever expected
with patience the Queen's death(which might have been de-
ferred, for aught I know, as long as an old woman was to
be had)[1] but that, upon the survey of his own strength,he
found it much too weak to produce a better effect than
baiting and a provocation of the Queen, by drawing other
claims out of her bosom to spoil his affairs with England,
many others lying nearer her heart than the family of the
Stuarts, who, to keep his interest up,swore an equal love
to papist and puritan, for which neither had a stronger
caution than the good or mischief they were able to do him.
And this was not so well concealed but that some of
either parties were able to prove it; which he contradict-
ing in his future practice contracted the hatred of all
sides: the ordinary consequence of so palpable a dissimu-
lation.

Others,[2] out of a like delight they took in arraigning
the actions at the helm, said this man[3] had forecasted as
impudently[4] for his own as the state, it being notorious
that his father's wisdom and advice was a principal in-
gredient in the bitter cup filled to the Scotch King's
mother, and that her jury, consisting of a number of the
greatest and richest nobility, were so infatuated by the
hopes and fears he had cunningly spread in their way, as
to cry, 'Her blood be upon us!' (which I doubt is too
truly come to pass),whilst he laid out the price of it in
the purchase of his own advantage. But the most of these[5]
were worn away, or had lost their activity in the dull in-
firmity of age; neither was it congruous to a rational
justice or belief that James should call the son of a
guilty stranger to a severer[6] account for the death of his
mother than he had some Scots, yet in being, who were
known to have not only betrayed her but, by their daily
importunity, to have hastened her destruction. For a conclusion to all farther disputes, he[7] could fasten nowhere

---

1. Cf.Weldon: 'The wisest in that kingdom[Scotland]did believe the king should never enjoy this crown as long
   as there was an old wife in England,which they did believe we ever set up,as the other was dead'.(p.318.
2. Others: 'Paul's-walking politicians'.
3. this man: Cecil.
4. impudently: perhaps 'imprudently'?
5. these: the original sentencers of the Queen of Scots.
6. severer: 'severe' in MS.
7. he: Cecil.

The Lord Treasurer Cecil

with greater security to himself, though the nation perhaps might have been put in more provident hands. For, as I was since assured by a principal branch of this family, the dread he had of the mad and irreconcilable hatred of the people was the impulsive cause that King gave no better caution for the present restraint of the Scotch incursion and his own future deportment.[1] The Earl of Northumberland's sword not being so keen or prevalent as this man's wit, however his honor[2] was pleased to rant during his tedious imprisonment, which was but a sad retaliation for so great an obligation as that age apprehended the King owed him. I should blot out this but that his restraint and Ralegh's were effects of Cecil's cunning, who was able to refrain[3] or let loose his master's spleen as it suited his own revenge, being the first visible occasion that turned his[4] favor from flowing so plentiful into the bosom of Somerset.

He was lavish in his lust, the cause that this amongst others of like nature were sprinkled upon his grave:

> Here lies Robert Cicil,
> Composed of back and pizzle.

But if the temper of a wise man, by reason of a vivacity of spirits, be impulsive to this vice, or the drought it causeth in the brain be necessary to the production of wit, something may be concluded in his excuse. Though great hazard lies upon the election he made of his daughter-in-law, the Lady Katherine, Countess of Suffolk's child, with whom report made him familiar.[5]

---

1. Cf. O's *Memoirs of King James*: When James was proclaimed king in London, 'the Hopes of some, and Feares of the Major part, assisted by the prudent carriage of the *Treasurer* [Cecil], and ranting protestations of the *Earle of Northumberland* (that in all places vapored he would bring him in by the sword) had stopped their Mouthes that desired (in regard of the known feud between the Nations) he might be obliged to *Articles*' (Para.3).
2. his honor: Northumberland. He was imprisoned for fifteen years.
3. refrain: restrain.
4. his: James's.
5. O. means that Cecil's daughter-in-law may also have been his daughter.

King James

Was so impeded in the management of his limbs as if inspired by a chemist,[1] or had owned no more natural production than a Scot, the mother of the casten chicken,[2]
rather than a result of the embraces of the Lord Darnley
and Queen Mary, looked upon as the most beautiful pair
then extant. He was upbraided by a countryman of his to
be _____ in every organ, having use of nothing but
his tongue, which yet was Scottish, and so contrary set to
the motions within, as it was not easy to discover by his
word what time of the day it was with him in his heart.
All passions in him were very acute but those of desire
and grief, the latter of which he did not farther par-
ticipate than concerns his own body, bearing without any
considerable perturbation the pain and loss of his nearest
relations--yet deserved not the name of cruel, though some,
stumbling at Sir Walter Ralegh's block,[3] have fallen into
such a mistake of his complexion as to charge him with it.
A proof of his mercy is apparent in the multitudes of par-
dons he granted to all faults of what magnitude soever,
passing by many reflecting upon himself without notice,
that men[4] indued with his power do daily make mortal.

The Star Chamber proved ominous to many during his
reign, which he suffered rather out of love to the mulct[5]
(in which he would pride himself much, though God knows
little of it came to his coffers) than any delight he took
in the corporal punishment of his subjects; bidding the
Lords, as I have heard some of them say, be sparing in
their execution, how lavish soever they were in their censures; which being taken off the file, became destinative
to posterity, who fell under the same judgments but wanted
the mercy, so as those punishments, only then named to ter-
rify others, were after inflicted in the open streets; and,
if I am not foully mistaken, the late war grew from the

---

1. <u>inspired by a chemist</u>: created by an alchemist.
2. <u>the mother of the casten chicken</u>: syntax unclear. 'Casten' ('castern' in MS) probably means prematurely born (OED, 'to cast', III.20.b), hence feeble.
3. <u>block</u>: executioner's block, also impediment. 'Walter' is spelled 'Wattr' in MS, as it was pronounced.
4. <u>men</u>: 'man' in MS. O. may have intended either 'men' or 'many'.
5. <u>mulct</u>: fine.

King James

too-far-dilated extent and merciless tyranny of this
court, consisting only of a number of mean-born, ignorant and hungry Masters,[1] who devoured all before they
came to the ground that would not worship such an ar-
bitrary image in the King, as the clergy had inspired
with a divine right.

I remember one telling a courtier for news that
Auld Jamie[2] was dead. He suddenly[3] replied, 'The nation will be wretched if ever it come into such a condition as to wish him alive again.' Which I am confident should never have been, had not his poor son run
after weaker counsel than his own, and taken himself
bound to satisfy the expensive humors of etc.,[4] by
which he was left to the mercy of such an uncircumcised
number of men as, under an hypocritical pretence of re-
forming vain-swearing, and sanctifying the Sabbath, used
themselves the most serious, deliberate and destructive
perjuries, with the highest profanation of the name of
God.

He was so ensnared with the delights of peace as
he could scarce afford a soldier a good look: the abuse
of whom, and the mayor and aldermen, being the most ordinary traffic of his wits, which might have been better employed in hindering their future injunction[5] by
keeping the black melancholy dust of discontent from
falling upon city and country, out of whose money and
valor, like sulphur and nitre, proceeded the materials
of the war. Which he had the dexterity to adjourn till
the days of his son, by gratifying the eyes of the many-
headed monster[6] with the crushing of some that had been
instrumental in promoting illegal designs, it being in-
different to him what became of the bark, so his voyage
might be finished in pleasure and plenty.

---

1. Masters: 'Mosisters' in MS; possibly 'Musterers' (a military metaphor that would go with 'ground' in line 4.
2. Auld Jamie: 'ould Jemy' in MS.
3. suddenly: immediately.
4. etc.: O. uses this symbol, both here and in his published works, to indicate that something is being suppressed: here, probably, the name of Queen Henrietta Maria, whose taste for expensive court masques may be referred to.
5. injunction: conjunction (of the army and the City of London).
6. many-headed monster: the common people.

Gondomar, that famous minister of Spain, had taken the proportion of his humors so right, as he was able to make him tremble or laugh when he pleased. Which proceeded not so much (as some falsely supposed) out of fear of the
5 sword, as the Jesuit's knife, that could not be better restrained than by the Catholic king, through whose mediation he obtained favor with his Holiness so far as he was never excommunicated by any other fulmination from Rome but that, blunted if not extinguished, which[1] the nations
10 lay under at Queen Elizabeth's death.[2] And in this and other brokages of peace (a jewel he converted into a drug that hath poisoned all future happiness) more money was spent than might have returned the conquest of any place without profit, safety or ambition had led his desire. But
15 his fear had so mastered all other passions in him as, to expiate the discontent taken at his daughter's marriage with a Protestant,[3] he offered his son Henry to the Infanta. Who,[4] wisely foreseeing the generality of his people might look upon it as an idolatrous match, would not
20 thus be bound: which, with some other umbrages,[5] brought him to the cupboard at Westminster[6] some years (I doubt)[7] before nature called him. Nor may the journey Prince Charles took into Spain be in so much probability imputed to his love as his fear, the Palatinate being as far out
25 of that King's power to restore them, as it had been formerly distant from his will, which made the innocency, if not the folly of that action[8] so ridiculous as the gallantry of that nation scorned to take advantage of it. Imprudence in both Kings being the best reason I heard given
30 for his going or coming home.

    He did so overstock his forest, and restrain the inhabitants from disturbing the deer, though found in the corn or their meadows, as if hunting had been a calling,

---

1. which: 'with' in MS.
2. Elizabeth I had been excommunicated in 1570.
3. Princess Elizabeth married Frederick of Bohemia in 1613.
4. Who: Prince Henry.
5. umbrages: suspicions, annoyances.
6. the cupboard at Westminster: Westminster Abbey. See Introduction, p. xxx.
7. doubt: suspect.
8. that action: the Prince's journey to Spain.

rather than a recreation, and venison the richest commodity of his kingdom, and that he chiefly labored to advance, signing a warrant with more regret for a stag, than he made demonstration of at the passing twenty destructive monopolies, though known to prejudice thousands of poor Christians. His partiality towards these beasts being such as the owners of money and friends might cheaper kill a man than a rascal deer.[1]

He esteemed himself eloquent and learned: how justly posterity may determine out of his books; among which the Apology written to all princes is not to be counted, being the product of more pains than he was able or willing to take. The speeches he made were uttered with such a natural and magisterial boldness, as did astonish more than persuade: yet he never stormed Heaven by appeals, and, if at all, rarely made a religious profession instrumental to his ends. I confess the Catholics were still persecuted before every Parliament, but that was by the way of preventing the Puritan, that spent more time in loading of them, than easing the Commonwealth: by his means making them enemies, who had most moderation, wisdom and friends; against whom for the generality they[2] had little to say, but what did purely concern religion. And now they[2] have had their full swing in reformation, I would fain know who is the better for it.

The Earl of Hertford

Besides the fatality of his descent,[3] had such a competent proportion of love in the west as drew a court prejudice before his actions, so as he passed, to an unusual number of days, under the never wholesome aspect of his prince's jealousy, the occasion many traps were laid for him: which he evaded, his stomach being too little, or his advice too great, to be detained in them. Yet upon the family's committing that damnable original sin, in

---

1. Cf. *Memoirs of King James*: 'Nay I dare boldly say one Man might with more safety have killed another, than a raskallDeare ' (para. 53).
2. *they*: the Puritans.
3. *his descent*: he was the eldest son of Edward Seymour, Duke of Somerset, who had been Lord Protector under Edward VI and was executed in 1552.

mixing their blood with the Lady Arabella,[1] another unfortunate branch of the royal tree (that starves all but the top bough), King James endeavored to set the Seymours so far back in the sphere of honor, as to receive the earldom from him by patent next [after] Montgomery. A fall never known to be given a nobleman of England that had not, like Lucifer, traitorously lapsed from his obedience, and did so shake, by the newness of it, the whole firmament of honor, that such a tempest rose in the House of Lords as his Majesty was pleased to temper his passion: which could not yet be done till, by the poor Lady's endeavor to escape out of the Tower in man's habit, she had made herself subject to a closer restraint; upon which her death followed not long after, to the grief of the people, who would have exchanged King James for any woman living.

As for this Earl, though his Lady had long since granted him a writ of ease, I have heard, a desire to serve the feminine commonwealth scarce left him till her death, which it was thought he adjourned[2] by his daily labor in the gravel-pits, the result of which is extant in many of the walks he made at _____,[3] not far from Stonehenge.[4] The fashion of his clothes were so singular, being worn out of memory and use, that he appeared mean and ridiculous to such as were not thoroughly acquainted with the honorable linings: which[5] a strange serving man unawares of gave him his horse to walk. This I am sure of: an old courtier told me he rescued him out of the hands of pages, who were wont to strike men with their Lords' pantofles[6] which they attended with at the Parliament doors; taking him for a buffoon; but, however he went, his life was pleasant and acceptable to himself, though tedious to his fair Lady.

---

1. Arabella Stuart married Hertford's grandson, William Seymour, in 1610.
2. adjourned: delayed.
3. blank in MS; perhaps Amesbury.
4. Stonehenge: 'Stonewich' in MS.
5. which: the Earl's 'honorable linings'. The anecdote which follows also occurs in the anonymous Woodstock (III,ii), a play of the early 1590s.
6. pantofles: slippers.

The Countess of Hertford

Daughter to Viscount Bin[don], had, besides, as rich education in beauty and majesty of person as could be capable of mortality; her fair hair being of such an unusual length that, combed out, it would have performed that   5
duty to modesty which her mother Eve did, with far less probability, expect from figleaves. Though like a watchlid it concealed parts more useful, yet the strongest design could not but consume some time in contemplating the curtain before they drew it: which, con-   10
tracted into curls, made a commonwealth of love wherein all that only beheld her had a share, the rest a mere tyranny and were disposed of according to her will. Which proved fatal to divers young sparks, that lost the light of their own reason by gazing too much on this sun   15
of beauty, especially one,[1] who, finding the bright hopes she is reported to have cast upon him,[2] being mad in despair made away himself . The heathen goddesses, no less than the Roman saints, were but her shadows, it being impossible to limn an accurate beauty without borrowing of   20
something truly belonging to her. And if her life fell short in virtue, yet charity may be confident, the chemistry of Hell could not convert so angelical a shape into a devil.
   Like a diamond that wants gold to set it (her father 25
being more noble than rich), this extent of perfection came first to [be] fathomed by a citizen's son[3] that lies buried in the Queen Church, having then his dwelling where the Castle Tavern now is in Paternoster Row. I doubt not but this disparity of birth sat heavy upon her 30
spirits, thought more nice to the punctilios[4] of honor than fame, the cause that in her widowhood she exchanged the former-mentioned young citizen for the old Earl of Hertford, expecting as quick a return for title as she had made with the merchant for money to maintain it. The 35
hopes she had to take a third venture for content being,

---

1. Sir George Rodney.
2. A word seems to be missing here: perhaps 'extinguished' or 'false'?
3. 'Pranell' (O). [Frances's first husband, a wealthy wine merchant.]
4. punctilios: 'puntieous' in MS. Possibly 'punctos', or 'puntos', which also meant small points.

it may be, the most acceptable contemplation her imagination presented her with the day of their wedding. But the fatal sisters did extend this old life to so unusual a length, as the Duke of Lennox, marked by her eyes for her last owner, might have wasted the stock of an ordinary patience. The supplying of which made her omit no occasion or means that afforded any opportunity, though never so homely, to pay the use of his desires and receive a reciprocal gratification for her own, the which, if suitable to her love, could not be moderate. From whence she sustained some prejudice in her honor by those who think no provocation sufficient for women to break a marriage vow: but, if a theft,[1] the more excusable since taken not only out of an inexhaustible treasure, but one quite abandoned of its owner. Who,[2] like a dog in the manger, kept a sedulous watch to prevent others from making the natural use of that he wanted strength or stomach to employ; by reason of age, or a humor of change reported to accompany him to his grave, priding like Lucifer to see the fairest flower in the garden of nature so far to wither in his arms, as it might need a supplement from art[3] which, if at all employed, was with such neatness as it seemed rather to resist than cover the sad effects of time.

However she appeared to the two former husbands, envy could not detect her of miscarriage towards Lennox, after whose death she cut off her hair and put it in his grave, continuing ever a widow, which some censorious ladies imputed to a disdain of going lower than a duke, a title there was no room in honor for her to transcend, the highest place[4] being filled with a contempt of all things of that kind savoring never so little of the imperfections of age, into whose haven she was by this time not only arrived but had discharged herself of the greatest part of that beauty which had rendered her youth admirable, there remaining no more but the weather-beaten vessel that had carried her so happily about the world that she struck sail to few in relation to the two gaudy beauties,[5] of beauty and honor.

---

1. theft: 'thief' in MS.
2. who: Hertford.
3. art: cosmetics.
4. the highest place: James I, a widower since 1619. Arthur Wilson suggests (p.259) that she hoped to marry him.
5. beauties: probably a mistake for some other part of this nautical metaphor.

The Duke of Lennox

Being of the Scotch line, had a more eminent place in King James' fear than love: yet to take from him all pretence of returning into that nation, he did not only supply his wants, out of a number of projects and gifts to a great value, but added the title of the Duke of Richmond, with the stewardship of his Majesty's household, to which belonged a large diet,[1] besides the disposal of all places below stairs, and an absolute jurisdiction over the Green Cloth. He was of a princely carriage, wearing his beard broad and long, by which he seemed older if not graver than he was; adding much to the dignity of his person, against whose symmetry I did not hear the critic of that time take any exceptions. For his languages of French and Italian, he stood indebted to breeding and travel, being not much obliged from his birth for more natural parts than were ordinary (the concealing of which might yet be wisdom in him to lessen his Prince's jealousy), his inclinations pointing rather towards pleasure than covetousness or ambition. This I am sure of, that altogether he appeared as courtlike a peer as any the Scotch King brought with him, having wit enow to keep him above the contempt of favorites, though never able to equal their power, endeavoring for no greater share of his master's affections than was necessary for the accomplishment of his own ends, without much dilating it towards kindred or friends.

He shared his pleasure with many ladies; but none had so full possession of his heart as the Countess of Hertford, to whom he remained a most constant servant for many years, till the Earl's death gave him opportunity to bury it[2] in that of a husband. Nor did this pass without observation that few (if any besides himself and the Lord Mountjoy) took so much pleasure in wives that had formerly been their mistresses. It was an epidemical fault in those times to brag of the favors of women, to the most intrinsic part of them, from whence flew a report, some say out of this Duke's mouth, that Sir Thomas Lake's daughter, wife to the Lord Roos, missed a secret ornament few women want at her age,

---

1. *diet*: allowance for food and living expenses.
2. *it*: the name of servant.

which, upon dislike taken by this nobleman, was supplied
by some artificial thing (after branded[1] about by the
bawdy lawyers, in that famous, or rather infamous cause,
depending between her father and the Countess of Exeter)
under the name of a merkin:[2] nor was it in a more private
place than in the Star-Chamber, before the King and as
many of the best of England as the room could hold.

Lennox[3] was a known pensioner to the most Christian
King,[4] yet a Councillor of England; nor was this relation
peculiar to his person alone, but all the rest that owned
that title, to the very Secretary of State himself.[5] Yet
James is registered amongst the most pusillanimous Princes,
though less cannot be guessed from this[6] than that he con-
temned not only the strength, but also the wisdom and
strategems of the whole world besides.

He[7] avoided the hatred of this nation as far as his
own and the Court interest would give him leave, not appearing often if at all in the Star-Chamber, that den of
cruel lords, over which a planet hung malignant to all
lying under the fatal aspect of the Monarch's fury, yet
received benefit from the abominated monopoly of the pre-
termitted customs though he shrouded himself from much of
the odium, by suffering it to pass under the name of the
Lord D'Aubigny, who was to succeed him in default of issue
but [was] not of himself able to have contested with so
much difficulty as his patent met with, unless supported
by the Duke. He could not be wooed by any endeavor of
the King's to give so just an exception to his own nation,
as they might have taken, if, conceding to his master's
fears (which were never moderate, sometimes unreasonable),
he had exchanged his title of Lennox for that of Richmond,
the first hereditary, the latter but for life.[8] Yet his

---

1. branded: 'brandished', 'handed', 'bandied'?
2. merkin: artificial vaginal hair.
3. 'He or Marquis Hamilton, I know not which, was in Queen
   Elizabeth's time Captain of the French King's Scotch
   Guard' (O).
4. the most Christian King: the King of France.
5. himself: 'themselves' in MS.
6. this: the fact that James allowed his courtiers to accept
   foreign subsidies.
7. He: Lennox.
8. 'Granted, and that which much discontented, at first but
   for life; being a title owned as belonging to the Crown'(O).

wife, being English, and owning no higher projects than
to go first where the Queen came not in person, was during
her widowhood styled the Duchess of Richmond. He was so
much an enemy to the match with Spain, that on a day assigned for the advice of this King's ministers, a mere
natural of his, which owned a Spanish look, was dressed
in a high quellio,[1] and all things else suitable to the
mode of that nation, nor was the long rapier omitted.
And, so accoutred, he (according to the custom he used
when he wore a side coat embroidered with apes and owls)
walked melancholy alone, as if he had been going to the
porter's lodge for correction, as he often did. It was
my fortune that day to meet him, nor can I ever forget
the ridiculousness, no less than the strangeness of the
composition, he appearing, to all that knew him not, as
natural a Spaniard as he was a fool. Which few of them
prove, especially those I have met with, though much
short of such abilities as the suborned opinion of those
times awarded them, appearing at a closer distance like
watches, more grosser and rich without than within. All
which this innocent did really personate, to their short
hair and picked beards, thrusting out his head and holding it awry, as if he kept intelligence with the winds.
It was not well taken by the King, the cause he appeared
in that wise habit but one day, the invention being handed from the Duchess to her servants, till at last it escaped all memories - if that of Revenge[2], the Duke dying
not long after, the very morning he was to attend his
Majesty to the Parliament where the House of Commons
was to present their speaker, which ceremony was upon
this occasion adjourned for some days. Nor did the people forbear to mutter he was poisoned, though the court
imputed his death to a surfeit arising from the apples
of love, it being past question that his soul left his

---

1. high: 'hugh' in MS; 'huge' or 'high'? quellio: 'a set
puff' (O). [A Spanish ruff, or cuello.]
2. Revenge: O. may mean either that the Duke's death so soon
afterwards was poetic justice or that it was an act of
royal revenge.

body in his Lady's embraces; nor was it[1] unlikely, he
having long labored of a phthisic.[2] If any match were
happy, this was for the time it lasted, no desire appearing in either party but what was natural to themselves;
so much the more to be admired, because she was arrived to
that age which doth commonly wither the affections of men.

Marquis Hamilton[3]

Another pretender to the Scotch crown, was by the same
hand[4] muffled in the pleasures of England and had the
Earldom of Cambridge intitled upon him, in the right of
which title he sat among the Lords in the Upper House
during parliaments, and as one of His Majesty's Privy
Council in the Court of Star-Chamber. Where I have heard
him dissent from all the rest in the behalf of justice and
mercy, which, though universally trespassed upon, appeared
in no place so far neglected as within her walls, sticking
like a Jewish leprosy, till with her own distraction, she
had procured that of the whole kingdom. I have often
heard him in his speeches, both public and private, take
so near a cast to the matter, as the quickest expression I
have met with did never yet overtake him, or rendered
their conceptions plainer, though at the cost of treble his
words. He participated so little of the false and fawn-
ing breath his country is generally inspired with, that he
dealt both love and hatred above board, scorning to wound
under the embraces of a friend, or the skirt of any other
power than his own. To the observation of which his ro-
bust body, and magnanimous spirit did not faintly prompt
him, by whose assistance through that treacherous Court,
by the phlegm of others; William Earl of Pembroke, who
succeeded him in the Stewardship, having for many years
little to support him from the danger a too high placed
affection[5] had exposed him unto, but a multitude of foolish

---

1. <u>it</u>: Lennox's death.
2. <u>phthisic</u>: a term used for several kinds of lung disease.
3. Not a character in the play.
4. <u>the same hand</u>: the King's, which had also bought off Lennox.
5. <u>a too high placed affection</u>: See Introduction, p. iii.

followers, with the more prevalent love and fidelity of
this gentleman. He was close-sighted and, as I have
heard them observe, not unlike the King of Sweden, that
might possibly do it[1] with louder clamors and more ef-
fusion of blood, but could not cause greater consterna-
tion in the Emperor, than his Marquis did in the King
and his minions, puffing[2] in public with Digby and
Cranfield, calling this pedlar, the other Spaniard, besides many high conflicts I have heard whispered from
the Council Table; the occasion of a Junto, though not
publicly owned till the reign of unfortunate Charles.

His hot complexion and strength - better main-
tained with chines of beef and pork, on which he would
plentifully feed, than (he did often say) the Duke of
Buckingham could be with his dear cullises[3] and cor-
dials-- brought him more ladies' custom than he in safety could go aboard with. But, lest posterity should muster up among his faults that freedom then used at court,
looked on as the necessary consequence of wit and valor,
I shall leave this quality to his unhappy son, that far
exceeded him in it. A marriage with[4] whom and
Buckingham's niece was not impossibly[5] desired by the
King, and perhaps so much the more easily counselled[6] by
the father because she, being under years of consent, no
less than the young lord, might afford him an opportunity to break it: the King's evil diet exposing his
life to no less hazard than Buckingham's worse proceedings (by which he was become odious to all) did
his master's favor. Either of which was able safely to
dissolve it, upon one of their dislikes, the young
lord's especially, who had, besides a visible indif-
ferency for the person, other sufficient causes to

---

1. <u>do it</u>: make war, like the Protestant champion in the Thirty Years' War, Gustavus Adolphus of Sweden. 'The Emperor'
was the Catholic Ferdinand III.
2. <u>puffing</u>: behaving contemptuously, as when he took part in
the impeachment of Lionel Cranfield, Earl of Middlesex,
the former 'pedlar', in 1624. Digby was ambassador to
Spain for many years; hence the other accusation.
3. <u>cullises</u>: broths.
4. <u>with</u>: between.
5. <u>impossibly</u>: MS has 'possibly', but this seems to make better sense.
6. <u>counselled</u>: 'conseled' in MS.

render it invalid, though in reference to one of a far
less noble extraction.[1] Which the friends of the Marquis
rung so loud in taverns and all places where they came,
being more sensible of his honor than the danger his life
and fortune was exposed to in that venomous age, that it
came to be suspected by the Countess of Denbigh, who was
not yet able to catch his son single in any private place
which had no stronger bait to allure him than her daughter; therefore, in thought of a future reputation, the
Marquis's death was hastened. The cause appearing to be
poison not only by the symptoms discovered in the body
but by some of his servants who, used to feed no worse
than their master did, had the luck to follow him. After
whose remove the match was with some difficulty consummated, though little to the content of either, the lady
dying long before her husband fell under that unfortunate
hatchet made sacred by the blood of the King. I do not
here or elsewhere mention their honor of the Garter,
presuming none can imagine princes[2] of their quality can
want it.

The Earl of Suffolk

Was, upon the assumption of James to the English throne,
drawn from behind that cloud the severe hand of Queen
Elizabeth had cast over the whole family together with
the head, and better deserved repute, of the Duke of Norfolk. A title[3] in her time looked upon as ominous to
itself, but after, in the person of Buckingham, fatal to
the whole nation: it being impossible for a recorder of
truth to free his profuseness and evil counsels, with
which he both at home and in Spain seasoned the more do-
cile years of the Prince, from a great part of the calam-
ities he afterwards met with. At his first reception into favor, he[4] set upon this newly revived family so

---

1. less noble extraction: than his own.
2. princes: 'A title given in heraldry, and by strangers to all the Earls of England, because they have crowns used at their installments and funerals' (O).
3. A title: that of Duke, because so many had been be-headed - eg. the Protector Somerset, and Norfolk, who, at the time of his death, was the only Duke in England.
4. he: Villiers (later Buckingham).

fiercely as the Earl of Northampton made more haste out
of the world than he needed,[1] by cutting a wen that grew
on the inside of his thigh: by which he prevented the
same, if not far greater, mischief his brother, the Earl
of Suffolk, underwent, by holding the Treasurer's staff   5
so long, for which he had no pretence either in justice
or wisdom, seeing how apparently he had suffered it to be
abused by wife, children and servants, and all [that] had
any place in the Countess's love or his own affections,
so as the first day of January, the day of gifts in   10
Salisbury's time, was, during his possession of the
office, dilated over the whole year. Nor was it congruous to reason that a favorite but newly admitted and
as it were a virgin in the arms of a doting Prince,
should want the will, in relation to his future fortune   15
(not to be supplied, but from the Exchequer), or the
power, to wring the staff out of his hands not able to
manage it to the best advantage for himself, much less
for the King--who could not choose but punish the
father, especially after Coke's hyperbolical expressions   20
at the arraignment of those less guilty, to take men's
eyes off from the partiality shown to the daughter. I
have heard, Villiers offered Somerset and Suffolk to be
their servant if they would leave perplexing his for-
tune, now so far rooted as not to be eradicated by any   25
hand but his own. Yet the confidence the old man had
in the King's mother's blood, with which the pillars of
his house were sprinkled, and the opinion the Countess
conceived of her beauty, children and Fortune--so much
supposed her own as to refuse her nothing, to a mixture   30
with the royal issue - made them neglect such offers of
compliance as after could not be obtained upon their
knees, Suffolk being cast into the den of Lords,[2] where
no tongue moved for him but Chief Justice Hobart.   So
soon was the power of this Lord and Lady forgot by such   35
as had formerly employed them in the accomplishment of
their desires.

---

1. Inaccurate: Northampton died 15 June, 1614, at the age of
   74; James apparently met Villiers for the first time in
   August of that year.
2. den of Lords: 'Star Chamber' (O).

The Lord Roos[1]

Who inherited that barony from his mother, was by the Earl of Exeter, his grandfather, and Burghley, his father, sent to travel under the care of Mr. Molle,[2] a man exemplary for learning in England and no less famous in Rome for a tedious captivity he lay under in the cruel Inquisition-- reported (and that with much probability) to be betrayed thither by Tobie Matthew at the instigation of the Lord Roos, who apprehended him a curb to his pleasures, into which his own youth had at the suite of the place's example cast him, so as in a short time he became himself as great a captive to natural lust,[3] feeding his affections upon the barren and loathsome apples of Sodom till he lost all appetite to any more natural embraces, together with the love most men uncorrupted bear to the habit, manners, and diet of their native soil, which he buried wholly in that of Italy. Where he was observed to improve nothing but that stock of vanity his friends had shipped him out with, hoping by the air his mind might be changed; whereas he brought home so prejudicial a detestation against the meat, drink and apparel of England that no advice of friends, example of others, or the no less palpable than abusive representation of his humors on the stage,[4] could warp him towards any other habit but what his wit has riveted in his opinion to be most decent. The cause he was ordinarily followed in the streets by more boys than report, though very large, had the impudence to say he came behind. Yet he yielded to the importunity of others so much, because the barony was to conclude in his person, as to marry Secretary Lake's daughter, a buxom lady, and not likely to have her fertility interrupted by any fits, especially those of the gripings of conscience -though she presented that family with nothing likely to

---

1. The Lord Roos: not a character in the play.
2. Molle: 'Mote' in MS.
3. natural lust: so in MS, but O. probably meant 'unnatural'.
4. Lord Roos first travelled abroad in 1605. While there are many stage caricatures of the affected traveller, I do not know which one O. is referring to.

Sir Edward Coke

reach posterity but what may be wished forgotten, with
the whole carriage in the Star Chamber, where King James
was so comical throughout all the proceeding as might
have profaned the justice of a less corrupt court, or
the person of any prince but[1] himself; no words or expressions being spared, though strong enough to raise the
foremost[2] mortified modesty of a strumpet.

    The Lord Roos entertained, between a friend and a
servant, one then known by the name of Diego, who was
his _____, and by whose administration he took the
cordial which so foully recoiled as the whole city was
filled with the report of it.[3] But, to be serious, I
never saw man's teeth so set on edge as his Lordship's,
which made him not to relish the pleasures of our
English court, though in that age replenished daily with
more dainties, gallantry and beauty than the city of
Naples (the place where he had spread the scene of his
Earthly Paradise) was able to present her poorer Viceroy
during the highest of his puff.

Sir Edward Coke

(According to a coarse expression used by King James in
the Star Chamber) was one seemed to eat, drink and
evacuate nothing but law, without any mixture of conscience or civility, more seemly perhaps in cases concerning private right than when the lives of his fellow
subjects were become the argument of the Bar, where he
was noted to be as impertinently cruel in his aggrava-
tions, as unnecessarily bitter in his language: the
cause he often drew such replies from an over-exasper-
ated misery as did not seldom make him blush through a
tougher impudence than I ever yet observed the face of
a malefactor steeled withal. For having, besides his
own, the levities of his second wife upon his accompt,
discretion might have informed him [that] his small wit,
and weaker judgement, in relation to any science but that
of law, though highly rated by himself, could not upon
slighter disadvantages receive more contempt than he was
possibly able to return. Yet along his circuits, especially through Cambridge among the scholars (for whom
his own ushers were not seldom commanded by him to find

---

1. but: 'by' in MS.
2. foremost: 'fomost' in MS.
3. See, below, I,iv, 85ff.

them room) he could so lay about him with his broken Latin and bald conceits as[1] it might inspire the penner of Ignoramus[2] with greater absurdities than some thought the true nature of a comedy might duly admit. Which opinion
5 would soon have vanished, had they known the man in the places of Solicitor, Attorney-General, etc.

The common report voiced him a greater asserter of his own profit than his client's, it being usual with him to take large fees and fail then at their need, urging that,
10 if not more, to be due for his non-appearance on the other side. Which made such as knew him best esteem conscience, honesty and civility as mere strangers to his nature, as honor was remote from his birth, being a branch of a mean stock. And though some may say that, after his face was
15 set the other way and he become a judge, the copy of his countenance to all no less changed than the leprosy of his hand cured, yet thousands are alive can witness that both Benches labored during his sessions with as gross impertinencies, injustice and cruelty, as he infested the Bar
20 under the most single livery of a pleader: especially in relation to any he did formerly hate, or was in hope to obtain favor at the Court, or respect from the Parliament from these. Suppression, ambition and profit being the most notorious ensigns he followed. Made manifest by
25 King James, who to justify this opinion, common at Court of him, stopped his mouth for six weeks in Parliament. during his highest career against state abuses after his own shameful ejectment out of power, by but saying in the ears of some that he was a fit man to fill the then vacant
30 place of Lord Keeper. Thus vain and arrogant were his hopes, after so high a provocation given in peeping into the secrets of his Prince, and making public divers contents picked out of such letters as Somerset, not only minion but principal Secretary of State, had in his cus-
35 tody at the time of his apprehension.

His passionate desire to destroy the House of Suffolk, his enemy (for to say truth none was ever more abominate to the peerage than Coke), did so effuscate[3] his purblind

---

1. **as**: 'is' in MS.
2. **Ignoramus**: 'Ignorance' in MS, but O. means the play by George Ruggle, which ridiculed Coke. It was performed with great success before James I on his visit to Cambridge in March 1615.
3. **effuscate**: darken.

Sir Edward Coke

sense of honor, as he could not but discern the King's
faults from the Earl's, with[1] other foolish carriage at
the arraignment of Turner and Monson, which, though fitter to make the subject of an interlude than character, is
not to be omitted by any shall venture to write the life
of James according to truth: unpossible to be acceptable
to the generality, who have had their judgement forestalled by the misfortunes of his son, and both their miscarriages buried in the absolute slavery and ruin of the
nation. In the meantime, if any expect,[2] stranger
evidence may be found in my study to prove the folly of
this man, whose sufficiency extended not higher than the
Bar, may have abundant satisfaction from a late book
entitled the Cabala[3] where a letter is printed, thrown
in at his window by one thought no enemy to any virtue
he could lay claim to.

    He so much neglected honor in all his competitions
with profit as he did not only compound at a set rate
with Samon, his steward, for diet - to abate the expenses of which, he dined by 10 of the clock, and so in no
great danger to be oppressed by strangers - but continued till he died at Stoke Poges in Co. Bucks., a house
of his wife's, where his body was without much decency
kept above ground till his stock, and mean furniture
could be disposed of to best advantage; his plate,
which also came to him by the Lady Hatton, having been,
before I had the luck to be so well known to him, converted into the same shape in alchemy. Who[4] had remained
so long his wife that she participated more of his humors
than suited with her honor, or that of the family she
came from.

---

1. with: 'which' in MS.
2. expect: if any are impatient...they 'may have abundant satisfaction'.
3. Cabala: see Introduction, p.xxix, and Appendix: 'Coke'.
4. Who: Lady Hatton, who had taken away most of the plate again.

To the Reader Concerning the Following Play

I have heard the famous Rabelais penned his unintelligible rhapsody[1] (for which the press hath oftener groaned than any book of that kind she was ever in labor of) out of deep scorn and discontent to see so much worth as he had formerly seen, neglected: that ignorant juncture affording none able or willing to understand, much less reward, so immense a desert. I will not own his design, yet cannot utterly despair of his fortune, whose tattered gown is more honored at this day in Montpellier than his person was in his best capacity to serve the state. Which I should admire, if experience had not rendered it no prodigy for posterity to raise monuments unto such as their fathers had killed with contempt. Captain John Bingham that translated Aelian out of Greek,[2] and the predecessor to Skippon in the City Artillery, a man no less fit for practice, perished for want in Ireland. Sir Thomas Glover, consul at Constantinople, and made famous by so many grateful acknowledgements for courtesies done to his nation, did little better than starve. Owen, the epigrammatist and another rare decipherer of letters (whom I have often observed to walk and dine together with Duke Humphrey in Paul's),[3] with a number more (who had wisdom and parts rich enough to endow this nation with greater peace and plenty than it is ever likely to enjoy), yet were suffered to be devoured with the rust of want and contempt or forced, with learned George Chapman, write for the stage - that lies now under a heavier censure than any wise nation ever loaded her with, being to my knowledge the best tutor

---

1. his unintelligible rhapsody: Gargantua and Pantagruel were first published together in 1553; the first English translation, by Sir Thomas Urquhart, appeared in 1653.
2. Aelian: Tacticus Aelianus. His Tacticks were translated and published by Bingham in two parts (1616 and 1629 respectively).
3. dine with Duke Humphrey: go without dinner. According to Fuller, the expression arose because it was believed that the tomb of Humphrey of Gloucester was in St. Paul's, 'where many men chaw their meat with feet, and walk away the want of a dinner' - but in fact the tomb in question is that of someone else and Humphrey is buried at St. Albans (Worthies of England, p.198.)

our ignorant gentry and nobility had: so as, if our
divines could have played their parts in the pulpit with
as much reason and eloquency as some of our poets cried
up morality on the theatre, reason and allegiance had
not so easily abjured the kingdom.

If this be looked upon as too green a subject to
creep from under so crazed and dry a roof, I refer
them for an answer to that wise Italian, who urgeth
it as an argument of the strength and integrity of
his understanding that, being many years my senior,
he had writ a comedy.[1] Nor can it be looked upon by
me for less than an effect of Providence, that I
should be entire in body and mind, when he that loaded
me with misery died mad and rotten, leaving (notwithstanding the vast revenue our father gave him) as distracted an estate to his issue as his wife's covetousness and his own hath allotted for his two younger
brethren and their poor children. If the nice rules
of a dramatic poem be violated, I desire the reader
to consider how few have observed them, nay, how impossible it is for my memory. Neither did I ever venture this way before, nor had I done now, but that a
Frenchman[2] said in my hearing that there lived not an
Englishman able to digest this story into a comedy,
much less come hear one of his countrymen who had done
it already, though not published - as I intend not
this. Yet, if the other slip out first, this may
possibly overtake it, if not in drollery, in truth.
However, I gained a diversion from sadder thoughts,
which is all my present fortunes can afford me, and
the real cause of writing this, which cannot deserve
a sharper censure than I have given it, in thinking it
better deserving reproach from others than to be read
over again by myself and corrected.

---

1. I have been unable to find any such 'wise Italian'; it
   seems likely that O. is remembering a traditional anecdote about Sophocles, who was said to have defended himself against a charge of senility by reciting verses from
   <u>Oedipus at Colonus</u>, his most recent work.
2. 'Dr. Du Moulin' (O).

THE TRUE TRAGI-COMEDY

FORMERLY ACTED AT COURT AND NOW REVIVED BY AN EYE-WITNESS.

DRAMATIS PERSONAE[1]

The Court:

King James I
Robert Cecil, Earl of Salisbury, Lord Treasurer
Thomas Howard, Earl of Suffolk
Katherine ('old Kate'), Countess of Suffolk
Frances Howard, Countess of Essex   )
Catherine Howard, Viscountess Cranborne)their daughters
    (married to the son of Robert Cecil))
Henry Howard, Earl of Northampton, uncle of the Earl of
    Suffolk.
Edward Seymour, Earl of Hertford
Frances Howard, Countess of Hertford[2]
Lodovick Stuart, Duke of Lennox
Tom, his page
Robert Carr, Earl of Somerset, favorite of James I
George Villiers (later Marquis, then Duke, of Buckingham)
Sir Thomas Overbury, confidant of the Earl of Somerset
Sir Benjamin Rudyerd, a friend of Overbury
The Lieutenant of the Tower[3]

---

1. Not in MS.
2. This Frances Howard was a cousin of the more notorious one. O. avoids confusion by referring to her consistently as the Countess of Hertford, and to the Countess of Essex as Lady Frances or Frank.
3. Probably Sir Gervase Helwys. See Appendix.

Hangers-on and Servants:

Anne Turner, confidante of Frances Howard
Simon Forman, a Conjuror
His boy
A Scots Beggar
Stone, Queen Elizabeth's fool
Saddler
Yeoman of the Guard
Rat-catcher
A Jesuit ('Signor Con')[1]
A Poor Scholar
Davis, a Proctor
Bess Swallow   )
Nan To____ [2]   )Servants to the Suffolk family
Tom Tankard, the Butler)
Servants to the Earl of Hertford
Suitors to the King
Bishops, Doctors, etc.

---

1. See Appendix. It is not clear whether O. meant the Jesuit of I,v, to be the same one who appears in III,ii.
2. So in MS. Osborne may be hinting at a real person's name or at some obscene coinage of the Jonsonian type.

PROLOGUE

Our play may own a fortune few have had [1]
Freely to say the truth of _____ bad,
Which is the cause, we beg no pardon here [2]
For those to speak that lived not in the year,
Or other freedom lent to Poetry [3]
Of which she borrows all, but leaves to lie.
If some expressions here too fat do show,
Accuse the pampered times that made them so.
Nice use, not Reason, makes lust's terms appear
Harsher than murder, theft, or to forswear.
Within a court who spreads his scenes, must be
Tangled with filth or baser flattery,
And he that harbours all the truth he meets
Cannot avoid the fouling of his sheets.

---

1. Blank in MS: the most obvious reading would be 'good and bad', but it is hard to see why O. should have been unable to supply this himself.
2. An acknowledgement of the many liberties taken with chronology.
3. O. distinguishes between poetic license and falsehood.

ACT I

(I,i) <u>Enter King James, and after him the Treasurer, Cecil.</u>[1]

<u>King</u>. Redeemed from Scotland, where the midday sun
Makes but a twilight in more happy climes;
And where the throne is canopied with snow,
Adorned with gems rough Boreas[2] frames in ice;
Famous for deaths of kings, and hatching geese,   5
Which, like the people, drop from loathsome shrubs,
And in such plenty that the last are found
Through all the world to fill Bellona's top[3]
As cudgels do a fence-school, where they hurt
Not as religion but base lust direct,   10
Exchanging peace and plenty into broils
By the false alchemy Knox did extract
Out of the people's sublimated zeal[4]
That poisoned all it did project to save.
A trap which England may be caught in, if she grow   15
rampant and presume to wince at those pressures I
intend to gall her with--
Though far below the plague of civil war,
Which, by compliance, I will shroud me from,
Not weighing what impends posterity.   20
Nor can I less, to gratify my fame,
Than robe these gypsies, sprinkled with the blood
Of Mary, though[5] my mother, though her zeal,
Or something else, caused her to wish my death.

---

1. Perhaps Cecil is meant to overhear James soliloquizing.
2. <u>Boreas</u>: the north wind.
3. <u>to fill Bellona's top</u>: to supply soldiers for any war.
4. <u>sublimated zeal</u>: zeal refined by alchemy, not into an elixir but a poison.
5. <u>though</u>: possibly 'thought'?

25	This made my friends for to erect that scheme,
	But 'ware to wish to execute the sense,
	Which was by English wizards brought about
	So slovenly, I cannot but in shame
	Confound the nation, yoked so strait by laws
30	They dare not quatch.[1] Nor can they be exhaust--

<u>Treasurer</u>. --Sir, you may be mistaken; for, though you are
arrived to so immense a greatness, as your sub-
jects dare not shrink under an easy burden, yet
the cisterns in the Exchequer have no other
35 springs but drops from the laborious brows, and
out of the seamen's veins. To feed them, therefore, I most humbly implore your Sacred Majesty
to retain the love of the English, found the best
recipe, in the predecessor's long experience, to
40 quench the fantastic fulminations of his Holiness,
no less than the more judiciously mounted canons[2]
of the Catholic King; and, if not in pity, yet in
policy, to stop the torrent of your luxurious
bounty, and not to suffer your insatiate country-
45 men to drain it out by thousands. Otherwise,
that mass of revenues, though unto more than sufficient,[3] will become in your days, or your son's,
less than necessary.

<u>King</u>. Upbraid[4] not me with posterity, a lumber that be-
50 fits the care of the commonwealth, whose quiet it
principally intends, rather than theirs that owns
them--not bound to afford children other room
than can be spared with conveniency, nor longer
than they remain as screens to faults, not
55 mediums between the people and their predecessor's
virtue. Subjects being apt to think old men's
government tedious, that carry a young untried
prince in the bale of their affections. Which
made wise Philip the executor of his own heir,[5]

---

1. <u>quatch</u>: move, stir.
2. <u>canons</u>: with a pun on cannons.
3. <u>though unto more than sufficient</u>: perhaps, 'though until now more than sufficient' ?
4. <u>Upbraid</u>: 'Abraid' in MS.
5. <u>his own heir</u>: Don Carlos, heir of Philip II of Spain, died in 1568. It was generally believed that his father had had him poisoned, though modern historians do not share this view.

I.i   45

              judging it no less ominous to peace and   60
              plenty in the terrestrial than celestial
              orbs, to see the sun shine during the reign
              of a more experienced father.[1]

Treasurer.   I confess Prince Henry's name is mounted high
              by applause, but, I am confident, without the   65
              least mixture of ambition.

King.   Single eyes are too dim to see the ends of
              princes' jealousies. Therefore advise the
              young man, if he recover,[2] not to cast
              scorn upon Somerset, but remember, my assur-   70
              ance of those I adopt is no less, nor of a
              consequence farther remote from my good,
              than the royal issue, made mine by a more
              contingent faith.[3] And, in relation to
              liberality, it hath not run at waste more   75
              luxuriously (as you are pleased to call it)
              than towards your family. Therefore it suits
              not the wisdom you are famed for to call your
              father's sins to a fresh remembrance by cross-
              ing my goodness to others.   80
                 Which cannot see the natural sons of
                 Bruce[4]
                 Like beasts devoured by the southern
                 worms[5]
                 That still do prosecute the mortal feud
                 Their baser countrymen had quite forgot,
                 Sucking more Scottish blood than you
                 durst draw   85
                 When Ramsay switched your cousin[6] on the face.

---

1. sun and reign: obvious puns.
2. 'Which he never did' (O).
3. Cf. p. 7,n7.
4. Sons of Bruce: the Scots. Not by reference to Robert the
   Bruce, as might be expected, but to Edward Bruce (see
   Appendix).
5. 'The Scots being reported to be long lousy, after they
   came into England, not being able, by all the shifts they
   had, to alter their habit' (O). The comparison between
   Englishmen and English lice is continued to line 86.
6. 'Montgomery' (O). See Appendix: Ramsay.

| | They were limited to no number, nor can it be expected I should put a greater restraint upon my own nation than England did.
90 |
| | Therefore has it no remedy I see,
| | Till both these Kingdoms make one Brittany.¹

                    Exit King.

Treasurer. If this fag-end o'th'world must fall on ours,
           (Not seen by God when he pronounced all good),
           When beggars breed like locusts, then in showers
95   Are blown about by Providence for plagues,
           I'll raise my family by them.

(I,ii) Enter a Scotchman like a rogue with a paper and a child at his back.

Treasurer   What's here ?

Beggar: I have heard of a secretary that could neither write nor read,² but not a treasurer--though presaged of your successor,³ who shall let his wife
5   ride on the staff, with all her children behind her, as they say witches run a-hagging, till they meet in the Star Chamber. But to my business: the warrant is from the King for twelve hundred
15   pounds.

Treasurer. Twelve hundred lice.

---

1. Brittany: Great Britain, a title which James had been unsuccessfully trying to get Parliament to adopt since 1604.
2. a secretary that could neither write nor read: probably Sir Edward Conway, sent as ambassador to Bohemia in 1619; according to Wilson, his dispatches made James I 'break into laughter, and say in a facetious way, Had ever man such a Secretary, that can neither Write nor Read?' (History, p.133).
3. 'The Earl of Suffolk, guided by his wife, and after questioned in the Star Chamber' (O).

I.ii   47

Beggar.   If your Lordship wants a recruit of that number,
                to suppress your Neapolitan jaundice,[1] I am
                able to raise them out of my own family with-
                out pressing the assistance of any more for-
                eign relations than wife and children, and   15
                should be glad you would rest satisfied with
                so innocent a bribe--richer being conveyed
                unto you under the peaceable title of New
                Year's gifts.[2]

Treasurer.   You all love sauce, though you hate pig,[3]   20
                else you durst not prate thus. But what en-
                couraged one of so base an alloy as your
                habit[4] speaks you, to a suit of this nature?

Beggar.   I scorn your epithets, whose blood hath mingled
                with the crown of Scotland and whose arms do   25
                impale the Northern Lion--whereas yours dropped
                out of an ostler, your grandsire having picked
                corns out of the strangers' horses' hooves in
                the well-known inn at _____,[5] not far out of
                the prospect of your father's barony. But the 30
                promotion of this grant was the compensation
                of a favor I did the King before Elizabeth,
                his mother's fatal sister,[6] had spun out her
                tedious reign.

---

1. Neapolitan jaundice: 'Cecil labored long of the P[ox], as report charged him' (O).
2. New Year's gifts: 'worth some years many thousands' (O).
3. you hate pig: pig was, according to Wilson, 'not very pleasing and acceptable to the Scots nation for the most part' (History,p.154). Osborne tells how William Earl of Pembroke, in retaliation for James's having thrown a frog at him, 'did in requital cause a Pig (of equal disgust with the same Prince) to be put under his Close stool'(Advice, Pt.2,para.8).
4. your habit: 'better than he seemed, the story not being wholly poetical'(O). O.never explains who is lurking behind the Beggar's disguise. It might perhaps be Lennox or the Marquis of Hamilton; both were related to Scottish royal family and hence had the lion in their coats of arms (see the Beggar's next speech).
5. _____: probably Stamford, near Burghley House.
6. fatal sister: one of the three Fates.

Treasurer. I see it is not enow to be ridden, but we must be
35   spurred with the sharpest reproaches of the_____.
            You do not yet tell the cause, which must be known
            before I can part with money. Did you make his
            Majesty such a present of vermin, out of the sweat
40   of your family, as you offered me ?

Beggar.   Faith, he breeds enow of himself of all sorts,
            sizes and colors: the cause he is still grabbling[1]
            in his codpiece. Yet the mistress[2] to whose
            beauteous daughter you have married your son (in
            hopes to have an heir by the surer side), with the
45   rest of the beauties, take it for a high honor if
            they may but smell to his fingers.[3]

Treasurer. I may well bear your reproaches, if you be so pro-
            fane as to blaspheme your maker. But, till you re-
50   veal the considerable piece of chivalry done, that
            may deserve this sum, I can say nothing to this
            paper. Besides, I have gone below myself to ex-
            pect an answer with so much patience. Therefore
            be brief.

Beggar.   His Majesty, being frighted with a protestation
55   made at the Cross at Edinburgh against the Bishops,
            a place as infamous as Golgotha for murders, his
            royal trousers[4] were in danger of wronging, which
            caused the cutting of his points.[5] And I, being
60   the next merchant[6] of note, trusted him for a
            dozen, after half that number of my trade had de-
            nied him. The which commodity lying until now un-
            paid for, he--

---

1. grabbling: groping, fumbling. Other writers also mention this habit.
2. the mistress: the Countess of Suffolk. Cf. p. 19.
3. smell to his fingers: 'kiss his hands' (O).
4. trousers: 'very usual with him to foul himself' (O).
5. points: a lace or cord used for attaching stockings to a doublet, frequently used punningly, as in 'stand upon points' (be over-punctilious) in lines 65-6.
6. merchant: 'Scotch pedlars called merchants' (O).

I.ii

Treasurer. If these be your rates, you stand more upon points in Scotland than ever I thought by the curtailed Presbyterian Levites, whom I have heard spurn them[1] about the Church among the people, as the prentices do bladders, only to warm themselves into sedition.

Beggar. My generosity in trusting to the word of my Prince and public faith of his followers, not less than his gratitude, swelled requital to this proportion.

Treasurer. I doubt it will be more than he or his son will be able to take up, if this hold.[2] But, in case you give the King's warrant and confess a receipt of the full sum, you may be paid presently two hundred pounds. Else, I cannot do less, in duty to my place, than acquaint my master with the large difference between his bounty and the merit of the cause: His Majesty reckoning according to the Scotch account, where five pounds will scarce suffice to shoe a horse.[3]

Beggar. I am content. For if the King be informed what he hath given, my suit may prove as cold as his that got the grant of the Deanery of Dunstable, and another's monopoly for converting chalk into seacoal.[4]

Treasurer. Follow me. (_Aside:_) The rest is mine.

Exeunt.

---

1. them: points (of doctrine).
2. if this hold: if this sort of extortion continues.
3. Cf. Memoirs of King James, where Cecil is said to be aware that 'a pound, upon the Scotch account, would not pay for the Shooing of a horse.' (para. 29).
4. 'An ordinary practice at the Scotch first coming' (O).

50   I.iii

(I,iii)   Enter Stone, Queen Elizabeth's Fool, crying;
          Saddler, Yeoman of the Guard, Rat-Catcher, etc.

Saddler. I see the old play called The Antipodes[1] will never
          be off the stage in England: where the Privy Coun-
          cillors are made at sixteen, and pages at a hundred,
          where fools grow great by turning statesmen, and
5   politicians become buffoons to purchase bread or
          preserve themselves from being devoured by the can-
          kers that grow from the venomous bites of Fortune.
          But I pray, Mr. Stone, let me, your old fellow-
          courtier, participate of the cause of your weeping.
10   I hope your venerable podex hath not been disrobed
          by the merciless porter[2] for cutting patterns out of
          such lords' breeches and ladies' petticoats[3] as your
          too nice curiosity had found in conjunction, after
          the counties[4] were departed out of the galleries.

Stone.   I was cured of the disease of the tongue by the Ad-
15   miral,[5] who made me be whipped for calling him fool,
          a term that Walsingham and Cecil,[6] that were no ways
          capable of such a reproach, would have laughed at.
          Therefore, Squire Saddler, it is not so well. For
20   these uncircumcized Scots, more nasty and mangy than
          their ancestors the Jews were ever reported, say my
          coat is a flower of the crown, not to be worn by any
          but the King's own countrymen, though they know the
          English deserve it better, for _____, and that
25   it may not ill become His Majesty himself, if the

---

1. The Antipodes: a play by Richard Brome, first performed in 1638. Since the Antipodes were on the opposite side of the world from England, it was assumed that all their customs were the opposite as well.
2. porter: 'Pages and fools were whipped by the porter' (O).
3. petticoats: 'said to be done by Sir W.R. to his own Lady in the dark' (O).
4. counties: the gentry.
5. The Admiral: 'Nottingham' (O). See Appendix: 'Stone'.
6. Walsingham and Cecil: two of Elizabeth I's chief statesmen; 'Cecil' is the father of the Treasurer.

I.iii   51

project of selling the Cautionary Towns in Holland,[1]
and the sending his son a-wooing into Spain, go on.
Others suggest, my place ought to be executed by
commission, not being possible to be performed
suitable to the present rebus[2] by an ordinary   30
fool without adding an extraordinary knave.
And of these, Montgomery and Nottingham are of
the quorum. The first by descent from his
father, though the younger son; the last from
marriage,[3] having in his age rather chosen   35
Scotch horns rooted on by incest, as report was
pleased to fame them, than English (worn time
out of mind by his ancestors). And in case of
any extraordinary cramps arising from the crude
justice used in the case of Cobham, Grey and   40
Raleigh, and the blasphemy of making the Fifth
of August[4] an holiday for the deliverance from
treason of no more formidable consequence than
blowing up the Queen's apron (which was after
perpetrated by many, without other danger to   45
her husband or themselves but what opinion
imagined they ran in relation to their healths)--
now, upon such reserved occasions and times,
some lords learned in the art of fooling are
to come in play as sub-committees.   50

Rat-Catcher. I know there are choice enough; but who
are the men?

Stone. Imprimis: the Earl of Northumberland, who by
obliging the King beyond requital bought a
place in the Tower, where he served a double
apprenticeship, and may have made his son   55
free by his copy if he do not forfeit his

---

1. the Cautionary Towns in Holland: these had been given to
   Elizabeth as security against a loan; James had
   threatened to deliver them to the Spaniards if the money
   was not forthcoming.
2. rebus: puzzling state of affairs.
3. marriage: 'Sir Francis Stuart's sister, and allied to the
   King' (O). See Appendix: 'Charles Howard, Earl of
   Nottingham'.
4. the Fifth of August: the day of the unsuccessful Gowrie
   plot (1600).

52   I.iii

                    indentures to a _____.¹ Next, all
                    Elizabeth's old Council,² that assisted to bring
60   in this hermaphrodite in affection without cau-
                    tion first given to the nation.

Saddler.   It is well, if their brains be tart enough to
                    correct the fulsome melancholy that cannot but
                    fume from the chill cowardice and base treachery
65   shown in deserting the Protestants in Germany
                    who had made him their head--till they cut him
                    off (a shrewd presage),³ and clapped the French
                    King on, in the face of Christendom.

Stone.   These have power to call in, on all occasions,
70   Edward Zouche, John Maynard, George Goring,
                    Knights, with Archy and John West, Esquires--⁴
                    who must be in, and I exploded, out of a hatred
                    our new King bears to all that loved my dead
                    mistress.

Rat-Catcher.   I was her Majesty's most excellent rat-catcher
75   30 long winters, but now these more reverend
                    vermin have found a hole in my patent--which
                    Coke, being Attorney, did wilfully make--and
                    through that have turned me and my family a-
80   begging.⁵

---

1. Blank in MS. Northumberland was imprisoned from 1606 to
   1621; for his son, see Appendix: 'Algernon Percy'.
2. Elizabeth's old Council: 'Fortescue only opposed' (O). Cf.
   p.19.
3. presage: of Charles I's execution. Probably a reference
   to 1610, when Henry IV of France led a French-German
   alliance which James had been slower to support; O. may
   also be thinking of events of 1624-26, when France, under
   Richelieu, was the chief antagonist of the Hapsburgs and
   thus indirectly a supporter of Protestantism in Germany.
4. Wilson mentions Goring and Zouche among those who devised
   entertainments for the king (History, p.104). See also
   Appendix.
5. The Rat-Catcher probably alludes to Ralegh's loss of the
   manor of Sherborne; see Appendix: 'Ralegh'.

I.iv

Saddler.   After all my stuffing was beaten out with trust-
           ing, and I reduced to the halter and tree, a
           base Scot unhorsed me, who had not when he
           came to England leather enough to make a hood
           for a Winchester goose.¹   85

The Guard. We are turned out, the King being afraid to
           look upon us, pretending treason in our
           stomachs, and that he and his posterity may
           be blown up by the Budge² we convert into
           urine. In whose place are myrmidons³ so lean   90
           and little as if first hanged and then stole
           out of the Anatomy School--not unlike what
           Booker, Balaam-Lilly's Ass, shall be able to
           prophesy hereafter of a wench in the year
           1650.⁴ Therefore let us all join in a peti-   95
           tion that we may have pensions in lieu of the
           main chines and organ ling⁵ we used to line
           our sides with, that begin to hang in bags
           already like a nest of chins below the chops
           of the great Scotch lady.   100

Saddler.   We are willing to serve you, could it be
           without entrenching upon the dignity of our
           places, for the Rat-catcher and myself, be-
           ing esquires,⁶ cannot, without a declension
           in honor, join with yeoman.   105

---

1. a Winchester goose: nickname for prostitute.
2. Budge: 'Wine and beer so called that was allowed by the King to the household'(O). The name Beefeater derives from this custom. See Donne, Satire IV, which describes these giants and their 'Fine/Living, barrels of beef, flagons of wine', in the days of Queen Elizabeth.
3. myrmidons: warriers (the tribe that accompanied Achilles to Troy).
4. Probably a reference to The Dutch Fortune Teller, published in 1650 and attributed (falsely, it seems)to Booker. It contains a set of wheels which the reader could use to look up the answers to questions, mostly to do with love and marriage.
5. organ ling: a large variety of the fish called ling; prob- ably contrasted here with 'old ling', which was cheap salted fish.
6. esquire: 'such were so foolish as to take the title of Es- quire upon them in the country, though not at Court, where they had no place of honor, but rather the contrary'(O).

Stone. I stand upon no such punctilio, though of the ancient extraction.

The Guard. Let's petition by ourselves, and leave Squire Saddler to sell pippins at that door where he quitted his fidelity for former arrears.

Exeunt Omnes.[1]

(I, iv) Enter the Lady Cranborne and her sister Frances, the day after her marriage with Essex.

Lady Cranborne. I see the air of Essex hath not altered your complexion: you do not look aguish this morning. Let me feel how your nose parts.

Frances. Leave gibing; you know I am no virgin, though I might live and die one for any account Essex is able to make to contradict it.

Lady Cranborne. I'll ne'er steer after the hulk of a drayman, if he be not full built in the gun room. Why, my mother voiced you in danger of spoiling, 'till Turner satisfied her with a reserve she had taught you, that would tip[2] all the equerries in the mews, and their horses to boot, whose strongest endeavours should not raise your countenance beyond the just proportion of a maiden blush.

Frances. Spoil me ? A bots on him![3] he's not able to spoil a doormouse or violate the chastity of a she-flea, being not rough enough during his highest tide to out-reach low-water mark.

Lady Cranborne. I have heard him pronounce himself owner of a lance able to rout a virgin troop, though raised, paid and inspired by the holy maids of London.

---
1. Exeunt Omnes: 'Exeant omnies' in MS.
2. tip: probably thieves' cant for deceive.
3. a bots on him: an imprecation deriving from the parasitic disease (the bots) which afflicted horses in particular.

I.iv

Frances.	A mere antic of gingerbread, that carries flames in the mouth but inclines downward towards the shape of a mermaid, playing on a bagpipe made of a broken reed.
Lady Cranborne.	Is he not a man ?
Frances.	No more than the back of your hand; there being as vast a difference between him and little Robin[1] (whom yet you know is far short of the perfect man) as 'twixt this and a cedar.
Lady Cranborne.	Hath he no mark of that wherewith required to incorporate a wedding bann ?
Frances.	Not thus much, in good faith; only a little puff-paste, such as you have seen garnish the haunch of a gelt deer.
Lady Cranborne.	How did he use thee ?
Frances.	Tousle, tumble and thumb me, as a dull, phlegmatic lubber doth his primer--but never able to advance a fescue[2] beyond great A, or 'in the beginning'.
Lady Cranborne.	If he cannot do your work, you must take in chare-men,[3] as my sister Wallingford is fain to do, and stamp his name on their labors, as it is foretold he will do hereafter by the speeches Sir _____ shall pen for him in the Parliament.[4]
Frances.	You need not seek farther for an example of that practice than yourself, nor a patience to bear it more prodigious than your husband, who hath yet something

---

1. little Robin: Robert Cecil, whose son Lady Cranborne had married.
2. fescue: a pointer used for directing children who were learning to read by spelling out letter after letter.
3. chare-men: odd-job men.
4. See Appendix: 'Elizabeth Howard'.

	to venture with you for a child, and might by chance
55	light upon one--as the tailor[1] did the thousand
	crown lot--by putting a half-piece, though it be a
	double cockpit-lay,[2] he never had the fortune. But
	mine is not able to contribute so much endeavour as
	might entitle him to a moon-calf.

Enter Mrs. Turner to them.

Turner. A fresh Hymen run to your rescue, armed with an in-
60   vincible weapon enchanted with the strongest charms
        of affection, upon the least dishonorable retreat
        this husband makes out of the list of your loves.
        And in the meantime let him daily invent new plays,
65   and every night act the pranks of some transformed
        deity, till he hath replenished your zone with a
        celestial shape.

Frances. Alas, Turner, Cupid was no bridesman of mine, nor a
         more real Venus assistant at my wedding than happier
70   nights suggested to my betrayed imaginations, Essex
         proving as barren as a rock which produceth nothing
         but moss and pumice.

Turner. Is nature turned cheater ? Why, his symmetry
        throughout proclaims him able to people a New
75   England with giants - not unlikely to bring upon the
        old and her governors the same restraint poets feign
        their predecessors would have imposed upon the gods.[3]
        So as[4] he could have taken up the nicest female com-
        modity city or country affords, upon the never-before
80   questioned security of his looks.

---

1. the tailor: 'in a great lottery intended for the advance of the plantation in Virginia, in which was got a thousand pounds, Sir Thomas Smith the projector, who, with Sir Baptist Hicks and many other famous citizens, sat whilst the lots were drawing in a house built on purpose at the west end of Paul's'(O).
2. a double cockpit-lay: a safe bet. (Frances means that Cranborne has a remote chance of hitting the jackpot, despite his small resources, whereas Essex has nothing to 'put' in at all.)
3. a passage looking forward to the Civil War, when the Puritans of New and Old England joined forces.
4. So as: 'so are' in MS.

I.iv   57

Frances.   'Tis confessed. Yet he is so poorly furnished
           towards the occupation of love, as, though I
           spared my beauties to the best advantage, and
           laid out more impudence than day or night ever
           before found me owner of, I could not mount him   85
           up to the least proportion of one able to
           gather the lowest fruits of marriage.

Turner.   I never affected these blind bargains. There-
           fore, I tried Dr. Turner's ingredients before
           I would become his patient for term of life.   90
           The omission of which makes great men hold in
           Capite] who are rather guardians than fathers
           to those that succeed them.

Frances.   Poor soul, I was so far from apprehending him
           upon suspicion of frigidity, that to render   100
           myself more acceptable I came to bed armed
           with a provocative, which, missing its natural
           way of evacuation, recoiled like that my Lord
           Roos took the first night he was to encoun-
           ter the roaring daughter of Lancelot du Lake[2]   105
           so as, if the maid had not been nimble, Essex
           had not lain barren for want of manuring.

Turner.   Eject him for not paying your rent, and I'll
           help you to one able to charge in all the pos-
           tures of Aretine[3]: who did so trounce your   110
           sister in law, that I was faine to swath her,[4]
           and, after some restitution received from a

---

1. hold in Capite: hold land or office directly from the King
   and hence be unable to bequeath it to one's heirs. A
   metaphor for cuckoldom.
2. Lancelot du Lac: Sir Thomas Lake, Principal Secretary of
   State from 1616-1619. See Introduction, Pp. xxii-iii, and
   'Lord Roos', pp. 34-5.
3. Aretine: Pietro Aretino, whose works are always cited as
   examples of pornography. The pictures for which he wrote
   verses were in fact by Giulio Romano.
4. swath her: possibly O. meant to leave a dash here.

115	caudle made of the gravy of nine legs of mutton, she swore she thought her kindness had been - . Yet she could not but cordially forgive him that did it.

Frances. For Love's sake, the man ?

120	Turner. E'en brave Somerset, who gave me after as neat a collation as ever I had from any, but my 'O brave Arthur'[1]. Yet he excused himself, as tired out by the old K---before.

125	Frances. I'll venture the rawest bit of him. And if he brings me to cry out or complain of my quarters, let me carry his knapsack for posterity. Having long since made his embraces the full circumference of all my desires.

Enter Old Kate [the Countess of Suffolk], Frank's Mother.

130	Kate. Morrow, daughters. You are catechising Frank how many courses her husband made at the ring Prince Harry took so often at Richmond[2] and whether the bladder brake and right in the nick so as his lordship could not but see in the morning the purse[3] of the pig (a trick fetched from Judea) with whose tail the witty Lady Haddington[4] made a frolic yesterday,

---

1. O brave Arthur: Arthur Mainwearing, with whom Mrs. Turner lived after the death of her husband, 'that kept Mrs. Turner and was said to be bewitched by her ['him' in MS] with his Lady' (O). 'O brave Arthur' was a popular ballad.
2. the ring Prince Harry took so often at Richmond: a common sexual pun on 'ring'. Richmond had been the palace assigned to Henry as Prince of Wales.
3. purse: 'the blood of a hurt deer a lyam-hound[bloodhound] is set to find' (O). No such use of the word is recorded in the OED. O's note is probably a pun on 'dear'.'Old Kate'is referring to some trick by which Frances hoped to convince Essex of her virginity.
4. Lady Haddington: Elizabeth Radcliffe, 'the Earl of Sussex's daughter and one of the wittest ladies of the time, which procured her respect from Prince Henry' (O).

I.iv   59

                    proclaiming it a true duplicate of the
                    evidence Essex had to show towards his   135
                    title to the remainder in fee of Frank's
                    maidenhead. At which they all laughed,
                    presaging it would be lost for want of a
                    legal entry.

Lady Cranborne.   All this is true, and a great deal more   140
                    his nurse told my father of. Yet he
                    would not believe he had King James's
                    Evil.

Kate.   What's that ?

Lady Cranborne.   Impotency of his members; having no   145
                    tackle fit to man out a weaker vessel
                    than a Suffolk pink[1] and therefore not
                    like to exchange his clyster bag[2] for
                    any better commodity than horns.

Kate.   What did he say for himself, Frank, when   150
                    he could not do withal ?

Frances.   He storied in my ears such prodigious
                    leaps, taken in Wales, from one moun-
                    tainous lass to another, and so unsuit-
                    able to the condition he lay in, as it   155
                    did convince him of a stupid ignorance
                    in all things relating to the feminine
                    gender.

Kate.   It might be an effect of a redundant de-
                    sire, as it happened to Tom Smith[3] who,   160
                    finding himself jaded by the Lady
                    Barbary's modesty, deserted her bed, and,
                    retreating to Duke Humphrey's,[4] rallied

---

1. pink: a small sailing boat.
2. clyster bag: instrument for administering an enema (and in this case, apparently, a sexual substitute).
3. Tom Smith: 'Baron of Strangford, who married the Earl of Leicester's daughter [Lady Barbara Sidney]' (O).
4. Duke Humphrey's: a brothel, 'a place famous for such cattle, and took the name from a tavern owning the head of the Duke for a sign' (O).

165	his routed spirits under the conduct of a brace of well manned W[hores], yet returned soon enough to whip out of his wife a young gig¹ before morning. Who hath left her Dutch husband an issue like a hodge-podge, composed of all nations and religions.
Frances. 170 175 180	This was inculcated till it grew as tedious as a repetition sermon,² with a number of philosophical relations more, backed with impertinent experiments-- as pissing through my wedding ring, crossing thumbs etc.--till I fell asleep tired, but not satisfied. As the Lady Ri--³ confessed herself only to be after the rebating of more several launces in one day than is reported of Guy of England or Amadis of France.⁴ Yet, after the fiddlers had awaked us by pronouncing that joy never like to befall me, he brought me to the old mumpsimus⁵ again, collected out of sorcery; concluding still to the tune of "Thomas you cannot"⁶, which I wished the music boy had changed to "Robin".
Kate.	Do you think he will not in time come to the use of his weapon ?
Frances. 185	Yes, if he that cast his horoscope be no farther out than in the Prince's⁷ He should one day hang against his King, distress him, and after all ship his fidelity to the other side in a packet boat.⁸

---

1. **gig**: flighty young girl, 'married to Sir Peter Rycaut's son, a Dutchman, but left him for change' (O).
2. **repetition sermon**: 'which used to be four hours long at Paul's Cross, and the most material part of four other men's sermons, besides his that rehearses' (O).
3. **Lady Ri--**; 'A most famous fair lady, but beyond belief libidinous' (O). Perhaps Penelope, Lady Rich.
4. Guy of Warwick and Amadis the Gaul, Romance heroes.
5. **mumpsimus**: old fogey, same old thing.
6. **Thomas, you Cannot**: the refrain of a popular ballad.
7. **the Prince's**: 'Prince Henry's fortune was truly foretold by a stranger employed by his mother, yet mistook in the death of her husband' (O).
8. This prophecy, of course, refers to Essex's career after 1642.

I.iv   61

>   But if ever he proves a woman's man, I'll be
>   h-----, and 'twere better I were, than to---

Kate.   Weep not, daughter. For, though a match of the   190
>   doting fool your father's making, against my
>   will, and your wise uncle Northampton's, I
>   shall keep you without steel from the green
>   sickness, which my namesake Stubbs[1] died of
>   rather than she would take a handful or two   195
>   of that which nature hath assigned for the
>   only cure.[2] And if with child, I doubt not
>   but the Essex Lion will, rather than the
>   Earldom should conclude in his person,[3] roar
>   it out for his own, in case he be not over   200
>   stocked, as he was that made away the brave
>   man in the Cupboard, and two girls buried in
>   Henry VII's Chapel,[4] though better bestowed
>   than another he married to the then master of
>   the great steel-yard at Heidelberg, whose pos-   205
>   terity have no other power of electing but
>   whether they will starve or live by the bene-
>   volence of others.[5] And the grandfather of
>   all these by the mother's side was no better
>   fore-handed than your husband, though reported   210
>   to be made far larger behind.[6]

           Enter to them the Earl of Northampton

---

1. Stubbs: 'whose life is in print' (O). See Appendix: 'Stubbs'.
2. greensickness: anemia, with loss of appetite, in young girls, who were sometimes said to crave foods like chalk and coal (and perhaps steel). The best cure for them, writers insisted, was a husband.
3. 'as it did' (O).
4. 'King James not pleased with so many children, having two daughters born in England but died, as Prince Henry did, not without suspicion of---' (O). See pp. xxix-xxx.
5. Refers (with a pun on 'electing') to Princess Elizabeth's marriage to the Elector Palatine (whose capital was Heidelberg) and the subsequent sufferings of her family in the Thirty Years' War. The Steelyard in London was the headquarters of the Hanseatic merchants.
6. 'Alluding to a vice I do not understand the gusto of' (O).

Northampton. 215	I wish you all joy, niece, yet could have been content y'had made a wiser choice in relation to power.
Kate.	So do I, noble brother.
Northampton.	Is the match repented already ?
Kate. 220	There is cause enow, God knows, for the poor wench, who is wrapped up in a map of misery and situated under a frigid pole, one side of her bed freezing whilst the other burns. Her pilot being as unable to quench it as Aetna, though as chill as the North-West passage. In power,[1] Essex hath neither head-piece, nor cod-piece.
Northampton. 225	She is too high built, and of too fair a stowage, to venture so long a voyage with one not able to pay her freight.[2]
Kate.	Prince Henry (God rest his soul) thought so when he named her the Bona Roba[3] of England.
Northampton. 230	It must be some prejudice conceived against her person, Which I'll endeavor to foment[4] by art: And if I can dissolve this match, no doubt You shall be pleased, and my ends brought about.

Exeunt Omnes.

(I,v)	Enter Signor[5] Con, a Jesuit.
Con.	I confess this island doth compass more felicities than the many nations my curiosity or mission have had me through. But with so

---

1. power: 'pore' in MS. Kate may be echoing Northampton's first speech.
2. freight: 'fraught' in MS.
3. Bona Roba: fine woman (generally used of prostitutes).
4. foment: encourage.
5. Signor: 'Segnior' in MS. He was in fact a Scot; 'Signor' must refer to his role as papal legate (see Biographical Dictionary).

I.v   63

>great an inconstancy in religion and
>weather, that they freeze in the same   5
>Church and clothes at even, they were
>ready to burn in during the midday of
>their Reformation. Which might have
>heretofore been palliated, if not cured,
>but that the priesthood swelled into so   10
>formidable an extent in power and number,
>as they suffered the Friars' zeal, the
>most ancient and becoming mantle of re-
>ligion, like the clothes of the laity, to
>be huffled with pride and fettered into   15
>ignorance that it is too thin to resist
>the storms of atheism, and [too] short to
>cover from inspecting Knowledge (now of
>late resolving to harken only to Reason)
>the nakedness of the trash that hitherto   20
>[had] lain under it. So as we are con-
>sumed in loading and unloading the interest
>of princes, to avoid the danger Peter's
>bark[1] hath been exposed to, since the
>curse of printing clogged her with such   25
>volumency of controversies, not to be
>avoided but by burning the--

>Enter the Earl of Northampton.

Northampton. Signor Con, give me your blessing as you
are a priest, and your hand as I am your
humble servant.   30

Con.   These are honors above my sphere from him
that was in orders[2] before I could sing
Mass, and had princes[3] of his alliance
martyred for the cause of Rome when mine
were not able to assist it with anything   35
but their prayers. In consideration of
which, together with your particular affection for the Apostolical See, I am by

---

1. Peter's bark: the Church of Rome.
2. in orders: 'Northampton thought to be a priest' (O).
3. princes: 'in the days of Queen Elizabeth, as adhering to the Queen of Scots' (O). See p. 12,n.3.

His Holiness enjoined to give you thanks for
preserving the Catholics from a total ruin the
Puritans thought to bring upon them through
their miscarriage in the Powder Plot, and to
assure your lordship that a Cardinal's cap
attends the least intimation of your desire.
Though not published in Consistory[1], to stop
the clamors that might arise in the next Parliament, who, by reason of your late book,[2]
look upon you as a beast of that flock Luther
taught to fleece their pastors and clothe
themselves with their skins.

Northampton. I pray, prostrate the humblest acknowledgement
may be imagined before his Sanctity. With this
assurance, that if it lie in my power to turn
my Master's Credo towards that aspect I ever
thought likeliest, to ripen his affairs [which]
the necessity of commerce hath planted within
reach of other princes, and free him from those
clandestine attempts this wavering condition
makes him obnoxious to, as well from the sinister schismatic as the right Catholic,[3] I
should blush to see so scanty a harvest follow
such pregnant favors as I have received. Especially the charge, given upon pain of ex-
communication, that none should accuse me,
though upon the rack, of anything might lessen
me in the king's opinion. Observed to the loss
of some lives, and hazard of more.

Con. Alas, a thousand of theirs cannot countervail
yours, in whom lies the richest bank of all our
hopes. Sir, I am also to inquire whether your
lordship hath received the Spanish gratuity for

---

1. Consistory: the ecclesiastical senate of Pope and cardin-
als.
2. your late book: G.marked this for annotation, but no note
appears in the margin, probably because he had forgotten
the title. He presumably means the speech against Father
Garnet, which was taken by Northampton's enemies as an
attempt to establish the sincerity of the Earl's Protestantism.
3. a pun on 'sinister' and 'right'.

I.v   65

             promoting the peace with that almost con-
             sumed nation by her[1] whose felicity ren-
             dered the Catholic cause no less miserable
             than her king.   75

Northampton. Yes, and have built a house in the Strand
             with it.

Con.   Is it not time to drive on the plot of
             your King's fomenting the German princes,
             by the mediation of Holland, to a rupture,   80
             and then continue to betray them, for
             want of supplies, since the Pope hath
             stopped all future practices and recalled
             his predecessor's Bull against him, for
             owning masculine embraces for most mon-   85
             archical, the other for common and demo-
             cratical ?

Northampton. It might be opportune in relation to any
             humor but his, whose concessions are as
             uncertain as his denials. Apparent in   90
             the order given to Wotton who proceeded
             before the Venetians,[2] during the inter-
             dict, with so many promises in his mouth
             as might have tempted a less advised
             State to an irreconcilable rupture with   95
             the Church, yet, upon the first intima-
             tion of dislike from Spain, a fearful re-
             cantation dropped out of his hose and the
             fault laid upon the ambassador, after sent
             for and made lieger to the boys at Eton   100
             lest he should tell tales. The result is:
             if ever he draws a sword in earnest I will
             not fail to eat the scabbard.

Con.   So do I. But the unfortunate discovery of
             that plot--in which so much prudence was   105

---

1. her: Elizabeth I (O. means 'that nation almost consumed by her').
2. the Venetians: a phrase marked for, but lacking, annotation by O. The Venetian Republic lay under papal interdict from 1606-7. See Appendix: 'Wotton'.

I.v

                laid out as posterity hath buried[1] in her fall
                all future opportunities to render her famous
                --hath given the enemies to Rome such plaus-
                ible occasions that, if the Parliament's spleen
                had been evaporated by words and laws, nothing
110   could have followed but confiscation and ruin.

__Northampton__[2] Nor could the King in Reason of State[3] deny
                his consent, though I know he will be so far
                from suffering them to be rigidly executed that
                he made them with no other design
115   Than to observe indulgent parents' ways:
                     Send sons to school, that they may beg
                     them plays.

__Con__   We have no protector but yourself to screen us
                from those firebrands,[4] the Puritan nobility.

__Northampton.__ I confess them so; but tied to such foxes'
120   tails as will carry them into their own corn,
                to the consumption of tithes, with all belong-
                ing to the Church; so that the knack of preach-
                ing will be out of frame for want of oil, or
125   make so high and insignificant a noise, being
                over-balanced by ignorance and power, that all
                will loathe it and turn in to the bosom re-
                plenished with peace and plenty.

                                  __Exeunt.__

---

1. __buried__: 'busied' in MS.
2. __Northampton__: Speech prefix added. MS has two consecutive speeches ascribed to Con. The inside information here seems more appropriate to Northampton.
3. __Reason of State__: 'ragion del stato', a term associated with Machiavellianism and meaning political (as opposed to ethical) motivation.
4. __firebrands__: a reference to Judges XV. 4-5; Northampton's next speech continues the Biblical metaphor and turns it into a prophecy of the Civil War.

ACT II

(II,i) Enter Mrs. Turner and the Lady Frances, in a disguise, like waistcoateers,[1] going to the Conjuror's.[2]

Turner. Madam, you are now past the pikes.

Frances. I am glad on't.

Turner. So am I, more for your sake than my own, such rencontres being usual with me in this walk.

Frances. Are you not afraid to cross the fields again ? 5

Turner. No more than the kennels[3] in Cheapside or the Strand.

Frances. The young fellow that accosted me was so rude, he would not let me pass without my oath: to meet me at a cake-house, I know not where, at 10 two o'clock, where he promised to make up the sixpence he put in my hand, twelvepence more, besides the expense of ale and simnels.[4]

Turner. A royal fare, and not often given by these suburb-clients, but upon strong affections. 15

Frances. How came you so well acquainted with their rates ?

---
1. waistcoateers: prostitutes.
2. to the Conjuror's: Forman lived in Lambeth.
3. Kennels: gutters. Cheapside and the Strand were the two largest streets in London, its commercial and residential areas respectively.
4. simnels: rich fruit cakes.

Turner.	I have made more than any cheating parishioner in London, for when I go disguised thus--as I do always to buy the best complexion belongs to your family-- I meet twenty customers that bid for my commodity.
Frances.	How do you get from them?
Turner.	If I like them not, I tell them they are mistaken, which exposeth them to so much scorn as they sneak away for fear of passengers. Else, I house with them in some sconce[1] about the walk, where the landlady shutting the door is taken for an infallible testimony of fidelity, and that she approves any design but leaving the reckoning unpaid. Condemning by this practice Rahab's predecessor,[2] for harboring of spies.
Frances.	I believe the ladies might meet as sweet, I am sure as sound, variety amongst these as[3] at Paul's, Madam Caesar's, or the Captain's wife in Aldersgate Street, that was the first who kept a male stews: whither the greatest shes in England came under pretence of eating apricocks ungelt[4]. Whose faces were so covered, or so disguised, as the traveller had nothing to boast of (an inconvenience not to be obviated but by making self-confession death) more than he could observe below the horizon.
Turner.	You'd never fadge with 'em. For, though I confess they have better stuff,[5] yet they cannot mould it so well to the content of a lady as your courtiers, who in the highest compliment can spin out time and observe all occasions to give honor content. (A rare

---

1. sconce: hiding place.
2. Rahab's predecessor: see Joshua, chapter II. O. means, 'Rahab, her predecessor'.
3. as: 'than' in MS.
4. apricocks ungelt: a common sexual pun whose meaning is clear from the spelling.
5. stuff: 'stiff' in MS.

II.ii   69

          invention my Lord Carlisle boasts he hath en-
          riched the nation withal--as if ignorant how
          to cure the feminine itch till the mangey Scotch
          taught us.) For, to say truth, these bumpkins   50
          are so upon the spur, that they set out before
          the more tedious women can break their fast.
          Besides, if you light into hands that delight
          in fingerwork, it will make you mad.

Frances. What discourse used the strong-docked[1] scholar   55
          that threw about his hands like the preaching
          buffoon doth in his juggling-box, when he
          plays Gog and Magog (the Fubs and Skelton of
          this age,[2] about whom the schismatics do so   60
          beat their brains as that they have put all
          into combustion through their description that
          suits better with themselves than any single
          person or society of men extant) ?

Turner.   He talked learnedly as you do now, at first: 65
          concluding it no less absurd for women to go
          without a man, than incongruous for one of his
          education to suffer it, who though but a Bachelor,
          had proceeded so far in the Art of Civility as to
          give me a jug of beer or appurtenant,[3] which   70
          was delivered with so much panting as a burgess
          doth a speech in Parliament when his notes are
          dropped out of his hat.

Frances. If we make no more haste, we shall be worse
          served in our return. There, pray, knock.   75
          (She knocks.)

(II,ii)   A boy comes and the Conjuror listens above.

Turner.   Is Mr. Forman within ?

---

1. docked: buttocked.
2. the Fubs and Skelton of this age: fool. A Fubs was a small, chubby person (OED); the poet John Skelton had become a jest-book hero. O. may have a particular preacher in mind - perhaps Hugh Peters.
3. appurtenant: that which pertained to it.

Boy   Yes, if he be not walked to take the air out at the
           chimney. For the doors have not been open this day,
           most of our intelligence creeping in at the keyhole.

Frances.   May we not exchange a word or two with him?

Boy.   I doubt not, till he hath some new ones. Which will
5   not be before the next great thunder, all his old
           having been spent to no purpose in rating the City
           beagles who, he presages, will run counter against
           all sense and reason, exchanging their money for
10   fetters. Yet if you will but tell me your business,
           I'll see what may be done, in hopes one day to have
           a turn with you in Via Lactea.[1]

Frances.   If I might purchase the favor, I would have my
           business, with the event, related by himself; it
15   being equally possible to know both, as one.

Boy.   Do you take devils for schoolboys, that you endeavor
           to pose[2] them? For my part, I would not, for all
           about you, with the addition of what may be extrac-
           ted from your vermilion, tempt a spirit with any
20   such questions of a thing known already, super-
           fluities being so contrary to their nature as they
           cannot be presented without danger to the operator.
           But, for what is no other way discoverable, we have
           them as ready as our Paternoster backwards, as,
25   that the English shall make a devil of their[3] king
           and that another out of the house of Ely[4] shall
           preach, fight, and govern without fear or wit.

Turner.   I'll be sworn, he told my maid I had the plate she
           lost, as plainly as if he had seen me when I laid it
30   by with an intent to bate[5] it out of her wages. Be-
           sides, it thunders; therefore, now we are come,
           let's not provoke these infernals but follow the
           course this Ganymede of Pluto directs you.

---

1. Via lactea: the milky way (but with a sexual double enten-
   dre).
2. pose: puzzle.
3. their: 'they' in MS.
4. another out of the House of Ely: Cromwell.
5. bate: take.

II.ii   71

Conjuror. above   I have enow.   35

Frances. Then, know, I am the unfortunate daughter of an
          Earl, thrown by my father's affections, not my
          own, into a bed so much the more loathsome be-
          cause emptied of all performance. Though re-
          plenished with as strong desires as ever filled   40
          the panting heart of lovers, yet the malice of
          Fate, as if she had not received full satis-
          faction for what sin I know not, hath fixed
          me to a foreign affection. Where I hang tor-
          mented between love and honor, two robbers of   45
          all worldly content.

Boy.   I will write a warrant for the spirit that
          haunts you and get my master to sign it.
          Who shall make him to keep the peace or com-
          mit him to Hell, till he brings a scrivener,   50
          a broker, and a Committee-man[1] to be found
          for his good behaviour. There being more
          current security with the merchants in the
          Stygian Lake than these blinking aldermen
          and foundered[2] Mayor are in London; from   55
          whence the farrier's son of Putney hath,
          and will, take away so many ounces of their
          silver, as they shall be in no other danger
          of falling into the staggers than what they
          are naturally liable to, from the heaviness   60
          of their heads. And for the repair of the
          husband's brick-works, you shall have your
          choice of any of the Five Members[3], already
          in our kiln, for propagating their own ends,
          instead of their country's.   65

---

1. Committee-man: refers to the numerous parliamentary com-
   mittees of the 1640s and 50s, the frequent butts of satire.
2. foundered: a condition found in horses. The term could be
   applied either to an inflamed hoof or to rheumatism of the
   chest-muscles. O. also uses 'blinking' (probably blinkered)
   and 'staggers' (a disease of horses and other animals), to
   link the animal-like Puritan City Fathers and the 'far-
   rier's son of Putney,' whose identity I have been unable
   to discover.
3. the Five Members: the members of Parliament whose attempted arrest by Charles I was one of the precipitating causes
   of the Civil War. Also a pun on 'member' in the sexual sense.

Frances.	Though my lord's chillness is construed a disease, and my no less hot affection to the other a scar to my honor, yet the first suits so well with my occasions and the latter is so becoming my affections, I should curse the hand that endeavored their cure.

To them enter Conjuror

Conjuror.	You lazy Rogue, if I had no quicker information from the stars, this Lady of honor might have waited--
Turner.	You see, madam, the Devil knows you.
Boy.	You are peeping under the coats of Virgo and might have proceeded farther than a boy's modest capacity is able to reach; therefore I durst not interrupt you.
Conjuror.	Get you in and set a chair for this Lady, or a scorpion shall twist your shoulders.
Boy.	I fly.

Exeunt Omnes

(II,iii) Enter Davis, a proctor

Davis.	Concupiscence that wastes others, immoderately used, keeps me thus plump and lusty. O, for such a prodigious leap, as Justice Granger took with his own daughter,[1] or an adulterous marriage like Mountjoy's with the Lady as rich in beauty as the more narrow-hearted sinners esteemed her poor in that [which] policy hath coined virtue,[2] to indulge my genius with sack and capons.

To him, Kate, Frank's mother, with the Earl of Suffolk, her father.

---

1. his own daughter: 'Whom I saw do penance at Paul's Cross, but he, being a cunning knave, denied it, and so escaped' (O).
2. A pun on the name of Penelope, Lady Rich. See Appendix.

II.iii

King.	I sent for you to be informed what cases of frigidity have fallen within the compass of your large experience.
Davis.	They are nothing so frequent as the results of heat; yet I have often been entertained by cold plaintiffs and defendants-- where ever proves a warm business.
Kate.	You know I have been a good and am not like to be hereafter an ill client to you. Therefore, I pray, upon your credit, acquaint us truly with your proceedings.
Davis.	Our credit is more famed for money than honesty, yet, upon this conjuration, I will be true to you. First, we squeeze all parties as[1] long as they will drop, before any considerable progress is made; but where purses are proof against fees and delays, the cause of defect is enquired into. As, whether it relates to a natural or diabolical Cause. If adjudged Fascination, a silly woman or two may be hanged, as in the case of the Earl of Rutland, who sent some wrongfully out of the world because his wife[2] was too honest to bring any wrongfully in.
Kate.	What are your proceedings in natural defects ?
Davis.	After incision made by the chirurgions, and inspection by midwives, etc., it will be no hard matter to make them swear there may or may not be cohabitation; and, according to their attest, judgment is given - if not obstructed by the mediation of money or friends.
Kate.	Say the invalidity respects the husband ?

---

1. as: 'all' in MS.
2. his wife: daughter to Sir Philip Sidney' (O).

                                                                II.iii

Davis.   Indeed, that's most frequent, women being oftener
            able for ten, than insufficient for five. But, to
            say truth, there is more partiality shown in the
            legal discussion of masculine infirmities than
5   theirs; the old judges voting any remnant suf-
            ficient. So as, if ladies had not a vast freedom,
            they might suffocate for want of --- which makes it
            hard for a wife to recover what belongs to her un-
            less he she mistook for a husband be so ingenious[1]
10   as to confess his defect.

Kate.   Can no trick be found to preserve the man's credit
            so far as he may willingly submit ?

Davis.   Yes, by laying only in the libel a Disability
            Quoad Hanc,[2] passing him by without aspersion in
15   relation to others. And in this case a Tester may
            be admitted for his trial as the Palatine of Rhine[3]
            had before the consummation of his match with the
            Lady Elizabeth, upon whose good or evil report he
            may be after famed.

Suffolk.   But what is left to the woman, to redeem her from
20   the foul imputation of an impudent ----[4]

Davis.   My lord, the less inconvenience yields to the
            greater, it being no shame to have a wife view'd in
            case of defect, therefore far less in justification
            of perfection. Besides, it is in the power of the
25   court to admit her scrutiny in the dark, or with
            her face covered. Of no small advantage, where
            penetration is legible, by suborning a copy of
            smaller prints.[5]

---

1. ingenious: ingenuous (the two words were often confused).
2. Quoad Hanc: with respect to this woman. See Introduction, p.xxi.
3. the Palatine of Rhine: Frederick, who married James I's daughter, Princess Elizabeth. A Tester, in this context, is presumably another woman prepared to test, and report on, the husband's potency.
4. Suffolk is asking about the effect of a public virginity test on his daughter's reputation.
5. a copy of smaller prints: a substitute who can more easily pass for a virgin.

II.iii

Suffolk.	Is she sworn?	
Davis.	Yes, in court--valued no more with us than the Oath of Allegiance, or a jig called in Scotland the Covenant.[1] The words bearing this sense: that her present husband never did nor, as she verily believes, never will, perform to her the duty of a spouse; therefore, she most humbly desires the honorable court to pronounce the marriage null, that she may seek due benevolence in a more pregnant bed, as is suitable to right reason and conscience. This being assigned, by law and custom, for the set form of a woman's Common Prayer.	
Kate.	I have as much as I desire. When occasion comes towards me, I shall employ none sooner than yourself to meet it.	
Suffolk.	In the meantime, take your fee.	
Davis.	I shall be no less ready than able to serve you. (Exit).	
Suffolk.	It were more suitable to your daughter's honor and modesty quietly to pass by her husband's infirmity, which might induce him to augment her jointure, and with more patience to bear a lapse, as my Lord Windsor[2] did from his wife, being made upon a like provocation.	

---

1. the Oath of Allegiance: required of all English Catholics after the Gunpowder Plot.
   the Covenant: the Solemn League and Covenant, which the Scots forced the English to sign in 1643 as the price of their support for the Parliamentary cause. It was a promise to establish a presbyterian form of church government.
2. my lord Windsor: 'not able to appear a man in the presence of a woman, though in their absence of most probable parts' (O).

Kate. 55	The world owns you for a Privy Councillor by your place, but 'God made you' is manifest in all your words and actions.[1] Else, you would not proclaim yourself wiser than the laity, not possible to be made the moulder of a remedy worse than the disease. Besides, wise men consider all disparagements arising from legal formalities as buried in the daily practice of the court, who, by imposing an unavoidable necessity, makes them signify nothing in relation to the scandal of any particular person.
60	
65	
Suffolk	They are your children, to be sure; therefore use your discretion. But for any part relating to me, it shall never be justly exposed to the question whose wife shall she be, since they both had her.
70 Kate.	Is this your religion, to sacrifice your daughter to a calf with a pocky face?
Suffolk.	I am resolved.
Kate.	So am I--that you are neither wise nor natural.

Exeunt.

(II,iv)	Enter the Lady Frances, Mrs. Turner and Conjuror
Frances.	Dear father, perform your promise and I shall not only make gold, the God of the vulgar, serve your desires, but, if it stand with your appetite, employ the best of my endeavors to congregate the loose spirits the chill winter of age hath dissipated in you, suffering you to charm them within the circle of these arms, impregnable to all other allurements but what come marked with the possibility of advancing my affections. In comparison of which, life and all earthly endowments are but trifles.
5	
10	

---

1. God made you: this seems to be a proverb (perhaps 'You are as God made you').Cf. 'God made him, and therefore let him pass for a man'. (Merchant of Venice, I,ii).

II.v   77

Conjuror. If he[1] do not leave his present honor and love
          of the King and future fortune to the guidance
          of those constellations which, like Castor and
          Pollux, twinkle in the firmament of your   15
          beauty, let me be ducked for a water witch and
          have my power confin'd to the charmings of
          frogs and blowing wind in the noisome tail of
          Lapland flyboats.[2]

Frances. Were this possible, how can the jealousy of   20
          Somerset be charmed, whose apprehension is
          fore-fed by the contrary reports running of
          my husband's sufficiency ?

Conjuror. To prevent which, take this image, created
          out of a mass of experience and informed with   25
          the most active spirit of a sympathising
          imagination, so as nothing can be applied to
          it that incites to lust or frigidity, but
          shall work upon Essex.

Frances. It can do nothing itself, can it ? For I   30
          have maids would make use of it, were it as
          little again.

Conjuror. Be sure none foment it but yourself. For,
          as the virility of that wastes, so will
          your husband's, and the other's love increase.   35

(II,v)   The bell rings within and the conjuror goes out
          at one door, and at another a scholar enters to
          them.

Scholar. Yonder are the coy waistcoateers again, which
          I will once more accost.
               Virgins, the wanton poet sweetly sings,
               Endeavor cannot cross the Fate of things--
          Therefore, since he hath once more cast me   5
          upon you, let's enjoy the creature,[3] and I
          shall equally divide my small stock between
          my wants and your own.

---
1. he: Somerset.
2. Lapland flyboats: witches (thought to be especially numerous in Lapland).
3. creature: creature-comforts.

II.v

Turner.	You undervalue yourself and overrate us, in offering booty for any commodity we can exchange.
Scholar.	If you will so far imitate the only pattern of your beauty, the skies, as to drop your favors gratis[1] upon a poor inhabitant on the foot of Parnassus, I shall study you for my eighth liberal science.
Turner.	May not a Scholar marry ?
Scholar.	Upon no slighter penalty than expulsion. Only, since the huge devastation raised out of the flames of Henry VIII's cod-piece, heads of houses are adorned with that privilege. Who were heretofore as frequent benefactors as they are now thieves; yet the better borne because given to the children of the Foundation.[2]
Turner.	We could not in charity deny one of the Muses' breed a course in our park, did not the fear of our keepers restrain us. Whose patience we dare not provoke by any longer stay in the purlieus, who may possibly meet us about this hour, no less to your damage than our own.
Scholar.	I look upon husbands as fools to confine themselves, no less than exclude others from what they have a propriety[3] in. Marriage being a result of policy, rather than nature. Yet my passions shall give way to your reasons, in hopes I may be able to palliate them till tomorrow by the applications of some philosophical mottos. At which time, I shall expect to meet you.

Exeunt several ways.

---

1. gratis: 'gretist' in MS.
2. Since the Reformation, the clergy have been allowed to marry, which means that they now receive horns instead of merely giving them as before. The point of this involved conceit is a pun on 'heads' of colleges--adorned both with marriage and with its consequence, horns.
3. propriety: property, proprietorial right.

II,vi,vii   79

(II,vi)   Enter a Pedlar with a Wench, a drum beating
            within.

Pedlar.   Hertford and his retinue are going to the
            gravel pits, for I hear the drum beat. Let
            Seymour the cuckold go dig.¹ Neither do I
            want a stomach to help him, could I yoke hand-
            somely with his heifer. Here he comes, but   5
            take no farther notice of him than overseer
            of the highways.² And be sure you keep your
            countenance, how ridiculously soever I carry
            myself.

Wench.   I'll play my game with such caution, as it   10
            shall not be easily discerned what I bear in
            my ace-point.

(II,vii)   Enter Hertford and his servant.

Hertford.   You'll ne'er attend the drum at six and three
            till cashiered, but back the maids when you
            should be upon duty. I hope by this the horse   5
            is ready, which will not carry your body so
            swimming as Roaring Meg doth, especially when
            you have two baskets of earth dangling at
            your shanks. Have you a mind the green sick-
            ness should be added to the scurvy pox ?   10

Pedlar.   Will you buy any Holland, cambrick, or
            Scotch³ ?

Hertford.   The ladies here trade with London and, for
            Scotch cloth, Lennox is bound to furnish
            our mistress so long as he owns a yard.

---

1. dig: with a double meaning.
2. overseer of the highways: the pedlar and wench are pretending not to recognize Hertford (cf. the anecdote told
   on p.24). As Lord Lieutenant of Wiltshire and Somerset,
   Hertford seems to be combining his military duties with
   his passion for gardening.
3. Holland, cambrick, or Scotch: kinds of fine cloth. The
   last of these gave rise to a pun (ll.13-14) of which
   Hertford is presumably meant to be unaware.

Pedlar. 15	He's out of the way, and 'tis possible I may have something she wants. Here is as fair an opal as ever lady of honor handled--warranted by experience to resist barrenness.
Hertford. 20	It must be as stiff and long as a l_____, for things of ordinary efficacy cannot swell her to the proportion of an ague-cake.¹
Pedlar.	The Italian duke that first pawned, then sold it, protested it did contribute as much to the generation of the French issue as Louis XIII.
Hertford. 25	If anything belonging to a Duke, Marquis, Earl, Baron, Knight, Gentleman, or Yeoman could have done it, the house you now see had not wanted an heir of her body.
Pedlar.	Would I were worthy to experiment my endeavors !
Hertford. 30	You have enough of your own to find you work, or I mistake your mark. Did you ever retail a child to the world by her ?
Pedlar.	No; yet 'tis not my fault, not the ware I carry, but the want of capacity for my parts and understanding.
Servant² 35	[aside] She'd fit yonder mouldy-headed gentleman to a hair.
Hertford.	You speak of Italy; were you ever at Venice ?
Pedlar. 40	Yes, and at Rome and Naples--where I met my Lord Roos, and Diego³ his man, reported to have rid so long with their faces towards the tail as he knew not how to mount before an English lady that stood⁴ for him in the Church, a market in which

---

1. ague-cake: an enlarged spleen or liver, caused by the ague.
2. Both this speech and the previous one are given to Hertford in the MS.
3. Diego:'a Spaniard, thought his factor in the Gomorrah trade' (O).
4. stood: 'told' in MS.

II,vii

	the priests sell worse bargains than the horse-coursers do in Smithfield. And from thence I came into Germany, where I spent many years in partnership with Leslie, till he gave off to follow the wars, being tempted from trading in small wares by a Laplander[1] that told him he should live one day to barter for his Prince.
Hertford.	[to servant] I have a desire to discourse farther with this witty pedlar. Therefore, dig your proportion, and to breakfast.
Servant.	[aside] You have a better mind to the pretty trull. I'm sure some doe-beggar will close his eyes in the park, and at one time or other advance him from her own to the bosom of Lazarus.[2] (Exit Servant.)
Hertford.	You have a tidy lass, Pedlar.
Pedlar.	A scanty gill;[3] one hath stowage for nothing but scraps from serving-men or the quintessence of a university commons.
Hertford.	Are you married to her ?
Pedlar.	No; we take one another's words, and by this avoid the great charge and more tedious troubles that less advised corporations have with their wives, it being lawful for me to exchange her for one more current in the general commerce.
Hertford.	Leave her here; she'll pleasure the town, especially if she be barren: the women being so overlaid with men, and their husbands with children, as they cannot peep out of doors for horns and debts.

---
1. Laplander: witch or sorcerer.
2. the bosom of Lazarus: Abraham would be more usual, but the fact that Lazarus was a beggar gives point to the change.
3. a scanty gill: pun on two senses of 'gill': a liquid measure and a familiar term for a girl.

Pedlar.   My consent must be a consequent of hers.

Hertford. You speak lovingly; come to the gate, and expect
          a jack[1] of the best.

Pedlar.   That's an experiment never out of the practice of
80   a chapman.

                    Exeunt Omnes

(II,viii) Enter Somerset and Mrs. Turner.

Somerset. A business of no less consequence than my life
           gives me the boldness and you the trouble of this
           importunate and unseasonable visit.

Turner.   O, the best of lords! I look upon you as the
5   apparition of my good angel. Therefore, say
          wherein so mean a creature may serve you, who re-
          solves to satisfy your desires, though to the cut-
          ting off half my days.

Somerset. Then tell me really whether Essex be in perform-
10   ance what report votes him; next, whether it lies
           within the reach of your mediation to procure a
           meeting with his lady, either here or in any place
           else that may promise security to both our honors.

Turner.   The Grand Segnieur may trust his magazine of
15   beauty as securely in the custody of Essex as with
          those that carry their--sticking in a turbet.[2] And
          for my Lady Frances (whom I presume still to call
          so, her husband not being able to blot out the
          marks of her virginity), I confess she honors my
          house often with her presence, but so far out of
20   the score of masculine assignation, as she will
          not enter if she hears any of the sex be there.
          Which proves Fortune a mere counterfeit, and not
          blind, else she and her lord had never met.

---

1. jack: a quarter of a pint of liquor.
2. turbet: turban (a reference to eunuchs in a seraglio).

II,viii

Somerset. Her eyes light[1] flames of love where'er she 5
comes, and the motion of her delicious[2] limbs
create materials to feed it.

Turner. As much might[3] be said for her husband, though
both found by experience as cold as the winter
quarter, being able, like the torpedo,[4] to chill 10
anything they touch.

Somerset. D'ye think her a virgin?

Turner. Yes, as immaculate as the lining of a Vestal.
Being innocent of all other natural pollution
than what she retains from the seed of her 15
fathers.

Somerset. Is't impossible to infuse a competent proportion of that invincible spirit into her by which
our court ladies are so strongly possessed that
they break the religious bands of marriage with 20
the same ease their husbands do those of honor
and probity?

Turner. I know not what such a Prometheus as yourself
may operate, the elegancy of whose language and
feature is not only able to inspire with love 25
an image of crystal, but render it active to
all human desires.

Somerset. I'll try my best receipts.

Turner. And if they do not work with her, ne'er a physician in town can. The danger is the patient's 30
being sick forty weeks after, else you might
practise upon all the maids in London.

Somerset. Let it be your study to purchase[5] an opportunity, leaving the success to my good or ill
fortune. 35

---

1. light: 'like' in MS.
2. delicious: 'delisheat' in MS; perhaps a conflation of 'delicious' and 'delicate'.
3. might: 'mought' in MS.
4. torpedo: a fish with an electric sting which had a benumbing effect.
5. purchase: 'purcher' in MS.

Turner.   She hath appointed to call here at four tomorrow,
            and if your occasions will permit then, I shall
            employ all my faculties to serve you.

Somerset.   The time I will punctually observe, only entreat
30   you to accept this. [He offers her money.]

Turner.   Good my lord make me not, though your servant, a
            mercenary one.

ACT III

(III,i) <u>A curtain drawn, and the Pedlar selling his wares to the servants.</u>

<u>Pedlar.</u> Pins and needles cannot bear my charges; 'tis lady-ware I live by. Therefore, my plump daughter of Eve, with thy iniquity under as green an apron,[1] I'll give thee thy choice of any bodkin here to show the Countess of Hertford this ring.   5

<u>Maid.</u> I accept of the employment, and shall show my skill, that it may pass without the least foil of prejudice.

<u>Pedlar.</u> I thank you, and will in the mean time endeavor to please the rest with a song.   10

[sings]

> Here are powders and drugs
> To repair the lugs[2]
> And noses the pox hath devoured,
> With ruffling[3] oils   15
> To recruit the spoils
> Of maidens that have been deflowered.
>
> For, though they have been
> Employed from thirteen
> Till thirty in both the foundations,   20
> From the minors in arts
> To the majors in parts,
> This is able to make reparation[s].

---

1. <u>as green an apron:</u> as Eve's fig-leaves.
2. <u>lugs:</u> ears.
3. <u>ruffling:</u> 'suffling' in MS. Meaning uncertain: perhaps 'stimulating'.

25	If any want gloves To draw on their loves With ribbons and lace to adorn her, Or a pretty disguise To cover the eyes Of such as you mean for to horn, Sir,
30	The pedlar's the man That furnish you can With all any heart can desire-a- But I leave for to sing, Because at the ring
35	Your lady begins to admire-a. (Exeunt.)

The Countess of Hertford enters and all the servants run away.[1]

Countess. How should a pedlar come by this ring ? Or who can justly accuse woman of inconstancy, since they inherit so much from men ? It was of too high a
40   value to be lost by negligence or made the price of a vulgar beauty, though a relative to nothing more worthy than itself; but, owning a power of a free admittance into a sole possession of all these graces--among which some have lost their lives,
45   others their wits, most their desires--I wonder at it.[2]

Enter Pedlar and Wench.[3]

Pedlar, I pray, how came you by this ring ?

Pedlar. It came to me; else I had never got it. We having many things sent us by gallants who had
50   rather be taken in adultery with our wives than trucking with a chapman for their father or

---

1. Stage direction: O. indicated the beginning of Act III at this point, but this must be an oversight.
2. The Countess is contrasting the ring's monetary value and its power to win her favors; for the effects of her beauty, see Appendix.
3. The 'Wench' has no lines in this scene. O. probably forgot that 'she' was there.

III,i

mother's commodities. Therefore we are
seldom able to cite the original, in whose
names we are for the most part ignorant; only
we enter the bringers with the price before
witnesses. This having cost me so much   55
trouble, care and vexation, as I heartily
wish I had never seen the owner.

Countess. You must tell or be compelled, for I foully
suspect you came not fairly by it.

Pedlar. I have a more[1] natural claim to it than you   60
can pretend to your beauty, though it would
not be taken well of a stranger that should
ask where you bought it.

Countess. I am sure 'twas not of you.

Pedlar. No--for I should out-blush that,[2] to have so   65
much poison found about me as you daily carry
in your looks.

Countess. You shall not swallow this gobbet, by all
your sauciness, without a better account.

Pedlar. Though confessed in your power, I stand as   70
free from fear as your ladyship doth from
charity to execute a revelation of that I am
shackled by oath from discovering. Yet, if
I should comply so far with the new doctrine
as to make necessity and self-preservation a   75
pretence for perjury, you would be angry with
what is effected by me, who stand in awe of
no man, much less the looks of a lady.

Countess. I will not, though I know it must prove[3] my
death for grief, or yours by law.   80

Pedlar. I am confident, the venture is of neither side
so great as we need trouble the assurance[4]

---
1. more: 'most' in MS.
2. that: her complexion.
3. prove: 'poure' in MS.
4. assurance: property insurance offices already existed in Elizabeth's time.

85	office, though it be rarer to hear a lady miscarry for constancy than a pedlar for uttering stolen goods.
Countess.	(aside.) The fellow's confidence makes me apprehend more in't than I am yet able to--Come, tell truth, and shame the owner,[1] who exceeds his tempter in--
Pedlar. 90	You must needs know where I had it: 'twas at the Castle Tavern in Paternoster Row,[2] rendered more famous by you than for wine and sausages.
Countess.	Was it pawned or sold outright?
Pedlar. 95	Exchanged to me for rich petticoats and the Seven Deadly Sins, wrought orris[3] which, if they were to be had, would suit your chamber rarely, especially the two large pieces of Pride and Lust.
Countess.	Who could vouch the sale?[4] For till that be known I dare bid nothing for it.
Pedlar. 100	If that be all, upon the return of it I shall be content. Yet you need not be so full of scrupulosity, for I dare say forty had a finger in it before me--as the nobleman reported of the lady it came from.
Countess. 105	I must reserve my patience, for I am sure to have use enow of it.--What lord was it?
Pedlar.	Faith, I have forgot, yet my own countryman.
Countess.	Was he not a Duke?

---

1. the owner: 'Tell truth, and shame the devil' was a proverb.
2. The Castle Tavern in Paternoster Row: a dig at the Countess's former marriage to a wine merchant at this address.
3. orris: variant spelling of arras, or tapestry hangings, which often depicted allegorical subjects.
4. vouch the sale: give proof that the ring was sold, not stolen.

III,i   89

Pedlar: So sure as I am a chapman, I know not. The
             King hath bred so many nits[1] of barons and   110
             lousy knights, that their titles are as hard
             to learn as[2] canting.

Countess.   (aside). This fellow's wit suits as ill with
             a pack as my fortune doth the affection I
             carry Lennox. From whom I doubt he is em-   115
             ployed, or knows my tongue is tied from any
             open prosecution, though I should find the
             ring stole. Yet I'll try what I can do.
             --Sirrah, you came not truly by it.

Pedlar.   Though my life depends on your will, a face[3]   120
             to one merely crusted with pomatum, as not
             to say my honesty is impeached- a jewel[4] I
             cannot afford you, who are reported to have
             lost it before nature had leisure to adorn
             the cabinet.   125

Countess.   Y'are a Scotch dog to use such language.
             If you yield not better satisfaction I'll
             have you tossed in a blanket.

Pedlar.   Europe affords not a female better under-
             laid for the purpose, than your honor, and,   130
             if you will experience that faculty[5] with
             me, the ring is yours.

Countess.   What baseness appears in me, to encourage
             such expressions ?   Or who hates his life
             so much as to prompt you to it ?   135

Pedlar.   This is you, 'will not be in passion'. The
             best is, a julep[6] might be applied with good

---

1. nits. eggs of a louse. Probably a pun on baronet (baron-nit).
2. as: 'and' in MS.
3. a face: something missing here ? -- the Pedlar seems to be comparing his bare-faced truth with her (as he insists) painted face.
4. a jewel: honesty, in the sense of virginity. Possibly a reference to the proverb, 'plain dealing is a jewel'.
5. faculty: possibly 'felicity'?
6. julep: a drink with a soothing effect.

		success, though yet unseasonable, till some other part is fomented to draw the distemper out of the region of the head.
140		

Countess. If you were ever christened, which may be doubted
of one of your profession, leave buzzing this about
me and fall to the business flatly; or, by the
hand I gave it to, honored next to my Maker's, I
145 shall be mad.

Pedlar. I thought you had esteemed none worthy of honor but
your self, which made me buy this picture (he pulls
out her picture) with an intention to hang it up
among such as trade out of the pure ends of gold
150 and silver.

Countess. I should defy these words, though uttered by the
oracle that I knew penned your speeches. Who did
then forget truth, else this ribaldry had been left
out of my scene. Though I wonder he could not find
155 a more apposite representation than a foul-mouthed
pedlar.

Pedlar. Indeed, a rat-catcher had been fitter agent to a
vermin that delights in gnawing men's hearts with
expectation and then bathes them in the corroding
160 brine of despair.

Countess. Who, I ?

Pedlar. Yes--you, that swore to be at court last masque.

Countess. I had other fish to fry.

Pedlar. What, country gudgens ? Your honorable neighbor
165 was shriveled into a spitchcock[1] long since by the
slim Lady_____, made downwards like a pair of
tongs,[2] and your usher's calves licked into bawds,[3]

---

1. spitchcock: a dish made with eels.
2. This presumably refers to the Earl of Pembroke, whose home at Wilton was not far from Hertford's Wiltshire residence, and to Lady Mary, his wife. See Appendix: William Herbert.
3. bawds: 'baudys' in MS.

III,i

| | disabled from following his father's trade for want of balls and a sound post, purged away in your antimonial[1] basin. | 170 |

Countess. Oh, the strength of cursed jealousy, that can shake into question an affection built upon so many assurances !

Pedlar. Had not I thought these complaints just, the crown of Brittany[2] could ne'er a' bribed me to the use of such language in so honorable a presence. 175

Countess. The unhappy condition of our births yields us up to scandal, uncapable of other confutation than Charity is pleased to extract from the improbabilities of vulgar reports grounded upon contrary circumstances. Therefore, to show how true a votress I am to that prince, long since made my idol, I did some months ago render myself his nun by cutting off my hair, in which, he hath been pleased to say, lay the strength of beauty. Which I still carried about me in hope to meet so trusty a messenger as I am confident you are, whom I beg to present it and so far favor truth, with[3] the disconsolate condition of a poor lady, as to assure him it was not torn off by the sharpness of his reproaches, but the sincerity of her affections-that would as willingly have sent her heart, but that she knew him confident it was his own already. 180 185 190 195

The Pedlar pulls off,[4] and appears the Duke of Lennox.

Duke. 'Tis here, and of more worth than the golden locks under whose custody lies the fame of Colchis. Madam, were all the deities provoked

---

1. antimonial: antimony is an element; a drink made from it was sometimes used as an emetic.
2. Brittany: Britain.
3. with: 'which' in MS.
4. pulls off: takes off his disguise.

200	the poets feign, half this would appease them: therefore I lay the sin upon your ram,[1] and do freely forgive all.
Countess.	So cannot I; who to this day was never upbraiding you with truth, much less to belch in
205	your face such noisome reports arising from the crude fumes of malice and envy-though not ignorant of the French Pip you labored of in Italy, not able to be delivered till Fenton brought you to bed in Smithfield; nor that the world owes the famous in-
210	vention of the merkin[2] to you--worn first by the Lady Roos, that gleaned most part of the ingredients out of your beard (naturally of that burnt color); and how you and the captain of the guard played for money at level-coil[3] with a market
215	wench, till your highest man run less than amb's ace,[4] yet endeavored to cog her judgment on your side but that she scorn'd to double with your partner although she swore you did so by her; and that--
Duke.	Nay, faith, madam, here's truth enow, in conscience,
220	to set against the falsehoods my furious discontent for your absence suborned me to utter: therefore, let me here stop your lips.
Countess.	My stomach would turn to salute my King in such a
225	dress.
Duke.	It is the same Jupiter, who bellowed for love of a mortal in a bull's skin, that we hear now thundering in the skies. Nor can it less suit with the elements of honor for a prince to become a pedlar,
230	for so noble an end as to enjoy the presence of his mistress, than a pedlar to be made an earl,[5] for no

---

1. your ram: Hertford (continuing the 'golden fleece' image).
2. merkin: see p. 28,n2.
3. level-coil: a game 'in which each player is in turn driven from his seat and supplanted by another' (OED). Here, a sexual variation on it (from French 'lever-cul').
4. amb's-ace: at dice, two aces, the lowest possible throw.
5. a pedlar to be made an earl: 'Middlesex, Carlisle, Hicks, etc.' (O).

	more generous a consideration than money, and a promise to betray his own corporation.	
Countess.	What little trull is that you peddle with ?	235
Duke.	Honest Tom, my page, through whose favor I got admittance - the old monkey having taken such an affection to him, that he hunts him about the park, and so muzzles him that he looks as if he were wattled.[1]	240
Countess.	You know my joys to see you leaves no room for anger, else you durst not abuse my--	
Duke.	Let's compound all within.	

Exeunt

(III,ii)	Enter the Earl of Northampton and a Jesuit.	
Jesuit.	The intimation of a Parliament hath made such umbrages in the minds of the Catholics, as I am bold to consult their oracle, your lordship.	
Northampton.	They are children in Reason of State; or, like weak conjurors, afraid of the spirits themselves have raised. It being impossible for them to be cured of their wounds received[2] by their own folly in making their shop lighter by a diffusion of learning, and then offering to the people more sophisticated Church-ware than the primitive ignorance, though far greater, was able to take off till all is put into the king's absolute power. Which many of the most	5

10

15 |

---

1. wattled: covered with wattles (flaps of skin) like a bird.
2. received: 'rec'd' in MS.

	popular members[1] have undertaken to do, out of hopes, and if they fail, the meeting and design shall dissolve together.
Jesuit.	Do you think the King would return to Rome if in his power ?
Northampton.	I believe him too wise to hold his crowns in fee of the Pope, as John of England did, or attend him bare-legged, like Henry the Emperor, or kiss his foot, after an excommunication; compliments too rank for the nice stomachs of this age, that are warmed with no hotter zeal than relates merely to policy. Upon which score, 'tis certain he may comply, and so become of one piece with his Catholic neighbors.
Jesuit.	Such a conversion might carry away more advantage from his Holiness than it brought, by tempting other princes to demand the like freedom, for whilst England remains in schism we can employ you as mastiffs either to fight amongst themselves or against any nation else appearing in a contrary form of doctrine.
Northampton.	This hath been made manifest to Tobie Matthew and Gage, but interest[2] and hope of the first performance[3] makes them blind and deaf to whosoever counsels. For, let our bishops post never so fast towards Rome, they will only carry the secular immunities, having the ecclesiastical wholly in their own dispose at home. And if they forsake marriage, the folly and trouble of which they begin now to take so much to heart (finding the evil consequence of children whom the wisest of them plant in other families), it will be thought sufficient compensation for all the protection his Sanctity can afford them.

---

1. the most popular members: 'At the Parliament in the beginning of King James's reign'(O). The Parliament in question is probably the so-called 'Addled Parliament' of 1614, which, largely thanks to Northampton's behind-the-scenes intrigues, lasted only two months and accomplished nothing.
3. interest: self-interest.
4. performance: possibly 'preferment' (ie. reward).

III,ii

Jesuit.	The Scotch nobility will oppose a reconciliation lest church land should revert, in which consists not only their fairest flower but their very gardens themselves.
Northampton.	They, no less than the English that side against you, are so obliged by favors, or obnoxious to law and poison, they do not wag but that way the royal hand will guide them, especially Pembroke, who, though he boxed the Earl of Carlisle at Marlborough, the same year the Judges fought in their circuit at Oxford,[1] yet his heart and his brother's [are] two lumps of strawberries making an island in phlegmatic cream.[2] Besides, he hath drawn his own process by writing letters and bawdy verses to one the law makes it treason to solicit-- though connived at in his age, where the distaff appeared more prevalent than the scepter.[3]
Jesuit.	Not to trouble your lordship farther in this point: if the King's design and the bishops' be only to make the first more capable of marriage and secure his treaties, having the Pope of an Umpire and the Clergy to gain the greater protection, whose maintenance hath nothing now to secure it but the bare affection of the king--a compliance in doctrine[4] will only undo stale

---

1. the Judges fought in their courses at Oxford: 'Jones and Whitelock' (O). Pembroke's treatment of Carlisle is described in an undated letter from O. to the Earl's chaplain (Miscellany, pp.192-3). I have found no other reference to Jones and Whitelock fighting.
2. phlegmatic cream: the rest of the nobility, by contrast with the more spirited Pembroke brothers.
3. See Introduction, p.(iii),i.
4. doctrine: 'doctaring' in MS.

85	chamber maids and cracked waiting-women, who, since Luther, hath taken the tribe of Levi for the lot of their own inheritance. We must put all into a combustion by fomenting the Scots.
Northampton.	Before you totally perplex the quiet of England, consider: his Holiness will be reduced to the condition of a chaplain if her power be added to the already unwieldy bodies of France and Spain, and of how much disadvantage, rather than benefit, the wars raised since this schism have been to the Roman See. No time being happy for the Church that affords freedom for disputation, her endowments being more in faith than reason.
Jesuit.	We must leave all to our superiors, whom, by my last letter, I find ready to recommend your niece's divorce to the grandees[1] of their party together with your desires of being High Treasurer. Concerning which, we have about this time a meeting, the cause I must take my leave.
Northampton.	Let me beg your thanks to the Consistory. (*Exit Jesuit*.)

Northampton Alone

<pre>
         I am no more a Papist than a Turk,
105   Farther than it conduceth to my ends,
         Which is my preservation, and desire
         To mount me to the Chair of Treasurer;
         Owning no providence beyond endeavor:
         For, though a workman may the chess-boards
110   make,
         Removes[2] are subject to the gamester's will,
         Since riches' lading swims not with Desert
         But bawling Impudence that plies the fare,
         Comes God's care short of Founders'?
115   Colleges enjoy for their indulgence
</pre>

---

1. *grandees*: originally, Spanish noblemen, but by 1649 a widespread term (for instance, among the Levellers) for any eminent figures.
2. *Removes*: moves in a chess game.

III,iii

>
> Remedies for ill, whilst he[1] restrains performance
> And yet bids us execute whatsoever he commands.
> Therefore my hands, soiled in the Powder Plot
> And after rinsed in Prince Henry's blood,   120
> Shall scape detection, if the match hit right
> Between my niece, and the King's favorite.
>
> Exit

(III,iii) <u>Enter the Lady Frances and Mrs. Turner in disguise.</u>[2]

Frances. I'll go no more in this habit to venture knocking down by all I meet.

Turner. Did not your marrow[3] do you right ?

Frances. Right or wrong, it was alike to him.

Turner. He I fell upon was so much a courtier as to   5
tell me he'd part with his birthright and render his desire servicable to mine, besides a world of excellent shop-compliments; only he brought them out as confusedly as he doth his wares.   10

Frances. Do you not know him ?

Turner. Very well, and so may you the other, they being both Viscount Campden's prentices, with

---

1. <u>he</u>: not clear. It might refer either to the King or to God. In context, Northampton seems to be talking about James's policy of double-think, but he is probably also making a cynical reference to the doctrine of predestination.
2. They are presumably on their way home from a second visit to Forman.
3. <u>marrow</u>: companion.

15		whom your family hath laid out many a pound for cloth of gold and tissue, before he traded for honor.[1]
	Frances.	I doubt he remembers my petticoat, for I am sure it is not yet expunged[2] his note-book.
20	Turner.	These citizens are used to handle such variety that they scarce know their wives' stuff, nor much look after it--being, as philosophers observe of cats, better acquainted with places than things.
25	Frances.	'Tis the more likely, because he made his approaches in such haste that he seized on my outworks without the least admittance to a parley, and, after dismantling, fell to storm as he had been mad. So as I am afraid the City is not with safety capable of so much scorn as the Court exposes them to; for, if they prove but half so fierce in the service of
30		Mars as they are in that of Venus, none but the Devil, and so base a son of Vulcan as shall be ashamed of his own name, will be able to put barnacles on their noses.
	Turner.	What if Somerset should take you up now ?
35	Frances.	He should be as welcome as a buttered bun were able to make him. For, being cover'd under this disguise, I could afford him more than in marriage I dare utter, for fear to be reported a bankrupt in modesty; suitors like mastiffs growing the
40		fiercer by resistance.
45	Turner.	His words to me did only intimate a hot desire to serve you, though I laid out the richest of my endeavors to buy out a mass of prejudices he came laden withal. In conclusion, he gave me a bribe to procure a meeting, which I did only promise to promote without the least undertaking of performance on your part. Therefore, if you meet, own it as a casual rencontre.

---

1. Viscount Campden (who did not receive that title until 1628) had begun life as a mercer named Baptist Hicks.
2. <u>expunged</u>: wiped out.

III,iv   99

Frances.   I shall-though confident he'll send to me
           before, according as the cunning man assured   50
           me: which let us go in and expect.

                              Exeunt

(III, iv) Enter the Pedlar's Wench and the Earl of Hertford

Hertford. I prithee, be not so squeamish. We are all
           of one piece, and those Fortune has dipped in
           a more orient dye are apt to be stained with
           detraction, which your more humble fate would
           free you from, though taken in the very act   5
           itself, whom neither Infamy nor Justice would
           prosecute farther than the tithing[1] extends.
           This made great Derby, though he were an Earl,
           bewail the loss of those his real pleasures
           enjoyed under the notion of a juggler.   10

Wench.   Have you not a fine Lady of your own ? Or,
           if enveigled by the humor of change, the
           world affords plenty adorned with birth,
           beauty, and apparel suiting your condition,
           whose pampered fortunes may have rendered   15
           them capable of more designs than you can
           possibly employ at this age. Whereas I own
           a heart as tattered with grief and need as
           these rags are by use and antiquity.

Hertford. I do promise to give thee that shall make thee   20
           happy. Though I look upon brave clothes but
           as gaudy curtains hung between our sight and
           the loathsome imperfections of great ones.
           Who sit all day hatching such diseases as
           quelquechoses[2] engender in them, the delight   25
           of fools that adore the artificial flowers in
           a petticoat and spurn with scorn at those
           more sweet and natural in the fields, pleased
           more with their show than substance. The

1.tithing: rural districts were divided into hundreds and
  tithings (which were a tenth part of a hundred).
2.quelquechoses: trifles, or triflers (here, probably, the
  foppish lovers of great ladies).

30	cause they court pomatum and diseases, planting their issue in a physic garden no longer fruitful than the Doctor's manuring it with noisome drugs and clysters. Which makes their servant carry the jug and the keg as cognizance of the antiquity of
35	their master's pox.
<u>Wench</u>.	If your Honor, wearied with more princely game, shall hold your resolution to stick so ragged a doe, I am resolved to stand you; but must desire to be spared some few days. Being, though at no
40	time worthy, at this most unfit.[1]
<u>Hertford</u>.	On Friday expect a fee.
	<u>He whispers to her, and then goes out</u>.
<u>Wench</u>.	A rot take you for a ram-headed Lord. If your prayers be no more zealous than your fasts, they are as full of sin as excess. Not a male under
45	this roof but hath laid earnest in money or meat, for ware that suits not with my budget,[2] though by importunity I have adjourned you to the end of the week, at which time they hope to feast their appetites--but what way they will convert my
50	fresh cod and poor-John into old ling,[3] I cannot imagine. But yonder comes my liberator.
	<u>To him the Duke of Lennox</u>.
<u>Lennox</u>.	You must presently convey my horse to the house where my clothes are, for the King is this night at Wilton.[4] And if he sees me not, the whole
55	Wardrobe will not be able to furnish clean clothes so fast as he will foul them out of fear I should be stole into Scotland, now the Marquis[5] is there already.

---

1. The 'Wench' is using the menstrual period as an excuse to put Hertford off.
2. <u>budget</u>: purse (with a double meaning).
3. <u>cod, poor-john, old ling</u>: three kinds of fish ('old ling' was salted and dried), with obvious sexual double-meanings.
4. <u>Wilton</u>: the Wiltshire home of the Earl of Pembroke, near Hertford's estates.
5. <u>the Marquis</u>: 'Hamilton' (O). (See Appendix).

III,iv

Tom. I am glad, for if I abide here in this habit I shall be consumed. It being a very Sodom, where 'tis nobody's lot to be honest:[1] men making as bold with their daughters as their cats, whom they teach to waul before others begin to play with their own tails. Not a weapon in the house but has been made at me. The Porter's a Swiss, and had broke in upon me but for my breaches, which I excused for want of clothes.

Lennox. How 'scaped you Hertford himself?

Tom. He's such an impertinent piece of fornication as would take say[2] of every hind, were the blood as ready as his handle.

Lennox. Did he give you no money?

Tom. Yes, a shilling when he roused me first, which he promised to make four when he broke me up. But the servants are so cockish they get up like witches every night upon the foulest hags I e'er saw out of Scotland, which they set like trusses of hay, now upon one end, then upon another; being able to afford males sufficient to keep rut in Hyde Park, yet leave stallions enough at home to horse all the west. If London bawds understood what trading's here they would not exchange their branded ware for the roundheaded balls which are as bald and rotten as the circle in Bloomsbury out of which the Portugal

---

1. nobody's lot to be honest: a pun on the name of Lot, one of the few honest men in the Biblical Sodom.
2. say: assay, a term used in hunting. The dead animal was 'broken up' by a knife slit, to see how fat it was. Tom continues the metaphor in his next speech.

ambassador's servants are cast, by couples, into the fiery ark of Cornelius' Tub.¹

Lennox. There's money to discharge my horses, and you, from farther trouble. Be gone.

90

Tom. I will, without looking back, for fear of being turned into a pillar of salt.

Exeunt.

---

1. **Cornelius' Tub**: sometimes also called Mother Cornelius' Tub, a sweating tub used for the treatment of venereal disease. The Portuguese Ambassador's house was in Bloomsbury(in the street now called Portugal Row), and Clarendon records a disturbance there in 1654. The ambassador's brother and some of his servants killed a man in a street brawl, whereupon the embassy was besieged by angry Londoners. By Cromwell's orders, all guilty parties, including the ambassador's brother, were executed. O. may be referring to this recent scandal, or to some other episode involving the Portuguese.

ACT IV

(IV,i)   <u>Enter the Lady Frances and Mrs. Turner.</u>

Frances The Conjuror is honest, for Somerset hath presented me this morning with a chain of pearl.

Turner. By whom?

Frances. The plump Lady Uvedale, that carries the sign of her calling in her face, whose majestical mouth is ascended by three steps and a half pace, wrought in a chin of sky-color'd marble.

Turner. I conjure you upon the penalty of honor not to fall in conjunction under her aspect--more malignant to love than that of tattling Apollos; apt, for want of other discourse, to reveal her own Venus, in which she is so prodigal to all comers, either in her particular interest or as a procurer for others, that, like those laboring fearfully of the rickets,[1] her husband thrives in nothing but his head.

Frances. You think she beats up your quarters--though you need fear no want of employment, if all the house of Suffolk should leave you but myself.

Turner. I cannot but look upon it as an illegal encroachment for her to operate in two so distinct

---

1. <u>rickets</u>: a disease which, because it wasted the limbs, was thought to make the head swell by contrast.

25	capacities of agent and patient, contrary to a Self-denial Ordinance.[1]
Frances.	Her house is haunted with the choicest company.
Turner.	A covey of forward ladies, I confess, jug there, but so old and diseased they carry ruin in their tailers.[2] Among whom are the merciful Kings-mills,[3]
30	with the Countess of Bedford, who, for want of quicker trading, drill Pembroke and Hamilton, two so bald buzzards who dare not seize on anything that lies not while they catch it.
Frances. 35	Retreat for a while; here comes Somerset. (Turner withdraws.) And if a woman was ever capable of reason, now Love inspire me with it.

Enter Somerset

Frances.	Happiness attend your lordship, who, I hope, comes on no more a dishonorable occasion than I meet you.
Somerset. 40	The height of my desires is only to see you and kiss those hands, which only have power to save, or kill, with a touch.
Frances. 45 50	And mine is (without farther notice of your civility) to acquaint your honor, I received a token from you; and though I know it far above any honest endeavors of mine to deserve, yet bearing the glorious title of your name no less than the magnificent image of your mind, I thought it not only beneath manners but the duty I owe to your personal merit and place you fill in his Majesty's favor to refuse it for the present. This, my Lord, gives

---

1. Self-denial Ordinance: the Ordinance of 1645, by which members of Parliament who also held military commands were compelled to resign them.
2. tailers: those who 'tail' them.
3. Kings-mills: 'Whose family is said to afford few valiant or honest' (O).

IV,i   105

             me hope you will not (if a fault) impute
             the acceptance to a slip in my honor--extor-
             ted merely out of a tenderness to yours--but
             remove all objections against both by a re-
             acceptance of that present which may possibly   55
             arraign you of prodigality, and me of light-
             ness. Therefore I humbly desire it may be
             given where there resides a greater probab-
             ility of requital.

Somerset.   It were sacrilege to recall a thing of the   60
             greatest moment after it had been offered at
             such a shrine, but, in relation to so poor a
             trifle,childish, though formerly owned by the
             Spanish Infanta, especially who[1] can call
             nothing his but what your concessions shall   65
             estate him in. And in my vindication from
             baser ends I protest to do nothing but what
             the Garter[2] I wear binds me to, which is the
             rescue of all distressed ladies. Among whom,
             story records none so miserable as those   70
             Fate hath cast into the barren arms of a
             monster.[3]

Frances.   If this be pronounced out of a sense of my
             sufferings I am obliged to be your Lord-
             ship's hand-maid. But if, participating of   75
             the vulgar error, you look upon me as judge
             of my husband's manhood, I could wish you
             better informed. Who may safely swear, if
             Essex had not himself been trumpet to the
             troop of defect report had mustered up in his   80
             charge and by which he did at first alarm my
             kindred, he might have inherited, with his
             honor and lands, his father's report in re-
             lation to women: my youth, then, and ignor-
             ance, yet, being too great to detect him.
             And if tears and prayers cannot rescue my modesty

---

1. who: ie. 'from him who'.
2. garter: 'The Knight of the Garter, among a number of
   other tasks, swears to rescue all distressed ladies'(O).
   For the 'monster' imagery here and in 11.61-64, below, see
   also Appendix: 'Chapman'.
3. then: in 1606, when she was first married to Essex.

85	from that strict scrutiny the hand of law (far against my desire) hath bound me to (she weeps), I doubt not but the world shall receive more satisfaction, than I can content, in so shameful a way of justification.
Somerset. 90	I am inflamed with your beauty no less than scalded with your tears, and shall never cool till I have wrought all to the same temper, that are able to help you.
Frances. 95 100 105	The grief sustained from the long extension of my honor upon the cruel rack of cruel scandal makes me snatch at so much hope from your courtship (as far out of my reach to answer, as power to deserve), that you may be tempted by your goodness truly to tell the king (yet otherwise persuaded, I hear) that nothing is more hateful to my mind than to appear a plaintiff in this kind; and that I apprehend no defect in my choice, having little to accuse my lord of but some unsightly demeanors which, if incident to marriage, imbecility may more justly be laid to me than him. Who am farther unable to endure them than my husband; else he would not be so frequent in their repetition.
Somerset.	If I do not (besides removing all prejudice from my master's breast) call him to your rescue from this barren rock (to which like another Andromeda I find you tied), let mercy be wanting when I ask it.
Frances. 110	I most humbly thank your honor, and will only load you this one request more: to accept a hatband, not as a requital but an acknowledgement of her gratitude, who owes you more than her life.
Somerset. 115	Though I esteem anything from you as a relic of a saint, I must refuse this, that owns the treble worth of what I sent you.
Frances. 120	I never weighed them together or consulted the opinion of a goldsmith; yet, if you will add to the rest of your favors the honor of wearing of it, I shall esteem these pearls as consecrated beads, and number my daily prayers on them for your prosperity. Else I am bound by a vow to return them presently.

IV,i   107

Somerset. Why then, I must.   Who shall ever offer up my
           obedience for a sacrifice to your will.   125

                    Enter a Page to Somerset

Page.   My Lord, a bedchamber-man attends you, who
           saith he hath been three hours in quest of
           you, and protests the king is so outrageous
           for your absence that none dares come near him.

Somerset. Though the scales of reward and punishment have 130
           for many years moved according to the propen-
           sity of my hands, yet the felicity standers-
           by imagine is not discoverable. The room of
           a favorite lying encumbered with endurances
           no less tedious than loathsome, kings being   135
           so remote from gods that they own more bestial-
           ity than other men, which makes their substi-
           tutes better able to perform a promise of in-
           jury than favor. The cause I desire your ex-
           pectation may not outreach the power of his   140
           endeavors who would no longer give way to a
           man's affections but out of hope to bring
           about those more natural.

              Exeunt Somerset and Page. Turner appears.

Frances.   Did not I play my scholar's prize well ?

Turner.   If you be but a scholar, the Devil must lay   145
           down the cudgels when you commence Master.
           I could not but smile to see how like a ser-
           pent you wriggled about him, whilst he stood
           gaping at the apples of your eyes, not seeming
           to value paradise in comparison of them.   150

Frances.   Art thou serious, my dear Operatrix ?

Turner.   As a funeral preacher, or a wench that, at
           Barley Break,[1] lies panting in hell, in hope

---

1. Barley Break: a game played in couples; 'one couple, being left in a middle den termed 'hell', had to catch the
   others, who were allowed to separate or 'break' when hard
   pressed, and thus to change partners, but had when caught
   to take their turn as catchers' (OED). Often used with a
   sexual double-entendre, as in Middleton and Rowley's The

155   to be saved by the meritorious activity of her
              sweetheart; not possible to be effected but with
              the breach of her couples.

Frances.   Never to be shaken off by me, till a virgin may be
              found out to supply my place in the scrutiny they
              intend to make after a maidenhead which, Love knows,
160   I did alienate before the course of nature had
              issued out the livery that makes us thought fit for
              possession.

Turner.   Madam, I have turn'd o'er so many female manuals[1]
              as might furnish a cabinet for the great Turk, but
165   find them either marked by their own fingers or
              adulterated with marginal notes like books at the
              second hand, not possible to pass undiscovered
              amongst any but scholars, and such as go drunk to
              bed. So as I have no hopes to fit you but with a
170   simple-headed[2] changeling, I have list[3] at the
              Dildo in St. John's Street.

Frances.   Haste to her, lest the heat of some Italian ---
              should chap her.

                              Exeunt

(IV,ii)   Enter Sir Thomas Overbury and Sir Benjamin Rudyerd.

Overbury.   Oh, the ill-suited fate of scholars, who, like
              University fishermen, have this commodity rated by
              a world ignorant of their value, in which a neces-
              sity is imposed upon wise men to follow the results
5   of such as carry no richer ornament than birth and
              the benevolence of kings have estated them in:

Changeling (III,iii and V,iii). O. may well have had this
play in mind, since it alludes to the Essex divorce (see
Introduction, p. xix); hence his use of the word 'Changeling' below, 1.125.
1. manuals: small handbooks (small, because Mrs. Turner thinks
   that only a very young girl could still be a virgin).
2. simple-headed: 'shimpladed' or 'shimphaded' in MS.
3. list: enlisted.

IV,ii   109

>   sweeping away, like generals of armies, more
>   applause from the dim prospect of a distant
>   danger, than falls to their shares who did meet
>   it by wisdom and overcome it in valor. Yet   10
>   such are not seldom neglected, without whose
>   better advice their masters' heads had been
>   lost in the fury of their prince or buried in
>   the softer impressions of a lady's lap.

Rudyerd.   Tom Overbury, judgement is outweighed by in-   15
>   terest, else you would not cry up a painted
>   Diana[1] feigned to have dropped from heaven but
>   known to be the wanton issue of peace and
>   leisure; ashamed to appear naked but before
>   such infatuate Actaeons, whose heads are   20
>   loaded and forked with insignificant argument
>   of no larger commerce than the pedagogical
>   tyranny extends to; noted for a rock in the
>   map of Turkey,[2] wiser nations esteeming the
>   walls of learned foundations as harborers of   25
>   schism, the cockatrice that hatches more re-
>   bellions than all the provocations tyranny
>   can invent, or, at best, but laborers for
>   mountebanks who, instead of curing natural
>   ignorance, insinuate a more chargeable and   30
>   unsociable madness; advancing learning be-
>   fore experience, without which it is at best but
>   a great blot: so vast a difference not being
>   visible between a scholar and a courtier as
>   you seem to discover in your Maker.[3]   35

Overbury.   'Tis one of the truths none are so impudent
>   as to dispute that Overbury's activity rather

---

1. a painted Diana: a false ideal of scholarship.
2. a rock in the map of Turkey: perhaps the Rock monasteries of the Cappadochian mountains? In his essay 'Upon the Government of the Turks', O. notes that 'The Turk finding Printing and Learning the chief fomenters of the divisions in Christendom, hath hitherto kept them out of his Territories'(para.71); he goes on to complain of the superfluity of scholars in England and the uselessness of most of what they are taught.
3. your Maker: Somerset. See Introduction, p. xxxv.

	than Carr's hath mounted him to this grandeur.[1]
	Else I should with patience endure till he fell in
40	a trap baited with an Essex hen.

Rudyerd. He hazards no more by loving her than a number, of
which some are of the same magnitude, others of
more age and wisdom; which renders the folly (if
any) prove excusable.

Overbury. If he travailed with no stronger affections than
45 men bear to a common,[2] in whose prospect and delight they are content to have sharers, my care
would be satisfied, in an assurance I have she is
wholesome; but he intends to enclose her by mar-
50 riage, to the loss of his honor, my preferment, and
love of his prince.

Rudyerd. Those in power will not admit it.

Overbury. You are mistaken, Ben. For the King promotes the
Nullity[3] by all the arts he can, having procured
55 the consent of most of the Bishops, in hopes by
this means to rid his fingers of Carr which have
long itch'd to be — Villiers.

Rudyerd. If he embarks in a voyage for his ruin, 'tis not
the averseness of your single breath can stop it.
60 Therefore comply, and do not cast away your own
fortune in an impertinent desire of the preserving
others, it being impossible to muster up any hope
in their favor, that oppose a natural, much less an
unnatural, lust.

Overbury. The King's honor and Minion's safety hang on my
65 tongue. Which no slighter consideration shall restrain than the breaking this match with Suffolk,[4]

---

1. grandeur: 'grandum' in MS.
2. common: a pun on 'prostitute' (cf. Doll Common in Jonson's Alchemist) and common, as opposed to enclosed, land.
3. Nullity: annulment of Essex's marriage on the grounds of non-consummation.
4. Suffolk: the house of Suffolk.

IV,iii

                    knowing enemies to me, and my preferment.
                    Therefore I am resolved.
                      Exit Overbury

Rudyerd.   Were not the brightness of this man's reason
            clouded by pride, he might pass amongst the
            most accomplish'd of this age; but his parts
            are so overrated by himself that he scorns the
            assistance of any remoter counsel than his own.
            This leaves his excellencies naked to the envy
            of equals, and his failings obnoxious to the
            jealousies of superiors, which I fear will ren-
            der his fall less pitied by such as know him,
            who have all lain under the sharpness of his
            wit or severity of his judgment.
              Exit Rudyerd at one door

(IV,iii)   Enter Overbury and Somerset at another.

Overbury.   A fancy of such a marriage were not decent in
            the heart of a prudent courtier, much less in
            his heart who hath the beauties of three king-
            doms to wallow his affections in, without
            yoking them up to a single Frank, already con-
            taminated by the possession of another.

Somerset.   Her husband did never enjoy her.

Overbury.   You have nothing but their words for it; too
            weak a security for a wise man to venture the
            stock of his posterity's repute upon, es-
            pecially having a full world to choose in.

Somerset.   I shall perish without her.

Overbury.   Fear not, my Lord. Such qualms proceed from
            an idle appetite to a thing supposed dainty--
            like women's longings,[1] which, once obtain'd,
            a few repetitions renders it loathsome all
            their lives after. Repenting their cost and
            labor, that might be abated, did they not make
            too great demonstrations of their desire:
            women, like hucksters, demanding more of
            strangers than such customers as know the

---

1. women's longings: cravings brought on by pregnancy.

value of that they desire to utter. Neither will the King refuse to drive on the bargain at a lower price than marriage (ever fatal to minions, if fortunate to any) who takes[1] as much delight in gazing on puppets as others do in their more natural use. Besides, women are so subject to leakage, that it exceeds discretion to be aboard longer with you, than wanton ladies are for physic at sea.

Somerset. You are a woman-hater and so are no competent judge.

Overbury. I protest I am not, but approve their use and commerce, as of silver and gold, though resolve never to make fetters of either.

Somerset. Were you ever in love, Overbury ?

Overbury. I have had an appetite to some certain women and eyed them with as fierce a stomach as children bear to strawberries and cream, but far from any danger of miscarriage in case of losing them. Never prizing a foolish longing so high as, like a conjuror, to contract my future hopes within the circle of another's will: sell freedom and immunities of my birth for a mess of white broth.

Somerset. Are not wives under as great, if not a more uneasy, restraint ?

Overbury. The same might be said of coupled slaves, whose love may moderate but cannot take away the tedious thralldom impending[2] wedlock: the fate of fools, and detestable to human nature. Which is cheated into this noose by Reason of State, that looks upon nothing for ill and severe that conduceth to the public good, converting that into sin, which our fellow-creatures do by virtue of an ordinance received from our universal Creator.

---

1. takes: 'take' in MS, but this verb refers to James.
2. impending: hanging ominously over.

IV,iii   113

Somerset. Is there no such thing really, in Nature, as
          Love ?

Overbury. No more than covetousness, or superstition:
          they being all products of a depraved fear and
          desire that suggests necessities where none   60
          are found but of our own making; and placing
          divinity in a creature set by Nature in a class
          of perfection below the thing that worships it.
          Not owning really the tithe of that delight
          which Expectation and Desire, the two broken   65
          Vouchers of marriage, are obliged to make good
          which, after fruition, vanish into counters.
          For, though women, like taverns, show glorious-
          ly towards the street, yet are they not com-
          municable nor afford that which welcomes the   70
          guests but through the mediation of a damp
          and unsightly vault or dungeon. Differing in
          this from wine: that the more you take, the
          less you are intoxicated. Neither are others[1]
          (though not so painted and authorised) unfur-   75
          nished of the same, if not greater delight.
          Therefore it cannot be vindicated from madness
          to bury your hopes in a tap house[2] out of whose
          circuit law enjoins you not to wander, how in-
          conveniently so ever you have situated your   80
          affections.

Somerset. Were all of your mind, the world would prevent
          Judgment[3] by making away with itself for want
          of a natural supply.

Overbury. Let men of empty souls fill it, who can farm   85
          out their strength for bread and consume the
          labor of their hands in making provision for
          the effect of another's lust. We having a
          weaker title to our heirs than to the curls of
          our hairs or parings of our nails, they being   90
          equal effects of an unnecessary redundancy in

---

1. others: both other houses (taverns had to have a license and a painted sign; ale-houses did not) and other women.
2. tap house: a drinking establishment in the area where debtors etc., were allowed to be at liberty.
3. prevent Judgment: anticipate the Last Judgment.

95	relation to individuals, like the seeds of plants that destroy the roots, no way sensible of the fate the next Resurrection runs. A philosophy known to all that lay not under the fascination of those red and white witches, a brother carrying more of our blood in him than a child, always a stranger on the surer side.
Somerset. 100	I am so stifled with the unnatural heats of the old King--that I would exchange it for any fire on this side Hell.
Overbury.	That might be done with less hazard than intrenching your credit on a common and borrowing another's engine to raise your horn-work.[1]
Somerset. 110	Sure thy father was a satyr,[2] and thy mother some ugly monster that conceived thee out of malice to beauty.
Overbury. 115	She was as other women are. But, since your Lordship's angry, I shall say no more, only desire you to compose yourself whiles my boy sings.

[Song:]

> They all do lie, that take a wife,
> Bound head to heels for term of life,
> Exposed to want, distrust and strife.
>
> For, say she holds out fair and good,
> A smile or word misunderstood
> May blot her fame and taint her blood.
>
> 'Tis youth and beauty's fatal hap
> To drop away into time's lap
> Which eats the bait, leaves us the trap.
>
> Opinion measures out desert,
> Proportioning to every heart
> What they think due that stand apart.

---

1. horn-work: a kind of fortification; here, used for the usual pun.
2. satyr: 'satire' in MS. Both words were thought to come from the same root, and O. probably has both in mind.

IV,iii

        Women like a Common Dock
        Or houses that have ne'er [a] lock
        Weakly secure their husband's stock.   135

        And if not dragg'd upon the stage
        By common fame or private rage,
        Yet loathsomeness will grow from age.

              <u>Exeunt Omnes</u>

ACT V

(V,i)   <u>Enter the King and George Villiers.</u>

King.   Love to men is seasoned with stronger delights
than that to silly women because pricked on by
the sharp spurs of restraint and rarity. Which
the vulgar affections, wanting, grows flat and
5   distasteful, like over-oiled herbs without
vinegar, maiming rational satisfaction for want
of confidence and discourse. The most elegant
ladies carrying no wittier arguments (in the
apprehension[1] of an imagination unsuborned by
10   fond formalities) than a dairy maid, yet strong
enow in both to confute desire before it is
able to consider the best way and means to resolve itself.

Villiers.   Though your Majesty's bounty in exalting me
15   out of the dregs of man, and placing me so near
your throne, no less than obedience as your
vassal, must stifle in me all opposition to
your will: yet, encouraged by the freedom
owned, with no higher presumption than is bor-
20   rowed from your goodness, I cannot but as yet
hold Nature for the best housewife of her own
stock.

King.   'Tis a truth, if considered of things in
gross. The happiness of whose creation
25   she destroyed by a too eager pursuit after
continuance, which, through an over-redun-
dancy in concupiscence, she hath dilated into so many millions of individuals that they

---

1. <u>apprehension</u>: spelled 'haprihention' in MS.

V,i

cannot with conveniency subsist, but by submitting to the tyrrany of Law and Custom, the inventors of sins and punishments: terms insignificant in her purer dialect till brought in by Reason, among a number of other confusions never to be obliterated, but by reducing man to such a paucity as the earth may nourish without being bounded by propriety.[1] Which this barren desire would soon accomplish, were it more epidemical.

Villiers. I confess your Majesty hath convinced my reason, though my sense stands stiffest for feminine embraces.

King. If I may enjoy my humor without impeachment of waste, you are left free to employ your talent either in the phlegmatic trade of Holland and other congealed climates or on the less dilated banks of warm Italy. Besides, I shall make it my business to intrust you in king-craft.[2] A taste of which you shall have in your neat removal of Somerset, who knows so much that, in policy, and for fear of the Scots, I cannot put him off without a manifest cause or take away his life in public, lest he tell tales. But, before things are better settled, conceal my favor, and comply with the Queen and Pembroke whom I have appointed to feed you.

Villiers. I shall observe your commands with all obsequiousness to your Majesty, and gratitude to them, who cannot be denied my raisers.
Exit Villiers

King. Not too much of that, it being my desire you should be the raven to pick out the eyes of them both.

---

1. propriety: private property (especially in sex). James is using the libertine argument that constancy in love is an unnatural, post-lapsarian requirement resulting from overpopulation.
2. king-craft: supposedly a favorite phrase with James; see Introduction, p.xxx.

(V,ii)   Enter Suitors

1 Suitor   Being your Majesty's countrymen and equally
           intending the good of your subjects, [we] do
           desire you to pass this patent.

King.   What's the contents ?

1 Suitor   "Whereas it is notorious to all the world
5   that the English nation is so degenerated
           in spirit and strength, that, contrary to
           her ancient prowess, she suffers all injuries
           and indignities at home and abroad, without
10   any remarkable notice but what is legible in
           her patience, which is most likely to proceed
           from an alloy of pusillanimity the gentry and
           nobles contract in their blood, by mixing it
           with City heirs and others of low extent:
15   these are for the future strictly to charge
           that none presume to make such marriages or
           contract[1] without licence first obtained
           from the Patentees, as they will answer the
           contrary in the high court of Star Chamber."

King.   I dare not grant it, for fear of causing an
20   combustion in the bundle of straws the House
           of Commons is shortly to be littered withal,
           who, if not the better managed, will set
           England on her head (the mirror of whose
25   government hath for many ages discovered to
           her neighbors their shame), and after brew
           up a worse tyranny out of the posterity of
           the rabble. (He speaks to other suitors:)
           But what would you have, with the long lean
30   faces that look as though they had been
           educated in Houndsditch or torn out of Foxe's
           Book of Martyrs ?

Suitors.   We desire a Parliament.

King.   If you will be a little patient you may have
35   a perpetual one that may give you occasion
           enow to employ more if you had them.

---

1. contract: 'contact' in MS.

V,iii

Suitors. Our aim is to elect such who, in their zeal, shall
         burn all Maypoles, that stand erected in our
         streets like so many lustful Priapuses belonging to
         the Whore of Babylon,[1] that man of sin whose flesh
         we long to eat, being great with the desire of re-
         formation.   40

King.   You shall have a warrant to the hangman for a
         haunch of the next Popish priest the Puritan
         beagles shall persecute to Hyde Park Corner, though
         it's confessed they and their whelps deserve to   45
         hold for term of life on the manor of Tyburn [more]
         than such poor Christians as suffer for their con-
         science. Of which the other retain no marks in
         their shops, or in the Church, but railing at
         Government.   50

Suitors. We will shake the corns of our feet against thee,
         in token of the hardness of thy heart, and then
         fly to Amsterdam, our new Jerusalem.
         Exeunt Suitors

King.   Who can deny Hell, that meets such spirits walking?

(V,iii) Enter Somerset to him

Somerset. The being you have given me will, with my shadow,
         be lost in a grave, if your power do not create a
         possibility of breaking the cruel yoke wherein the
         Lady Frances draws single, without any ease from
         her husband, the weightiest desire nature hath im- 5
         posed upon her subjects: the relief of oppressed

---

1. the Whore of Babylon: a term applied by Protestants to the
   Roman Catholic Church. Here it seems also to mean the
   Pope ('that man of sin'). The confusion of gender is
   probably meant to ridicule the Puritans' ignorant zeal.
   They go on to compare themselves to pregnant women 'longing' for a reformation - an image frequently used in the
   1640s. Some of the royalist pamphlets in dramatic form,
   dating from 1647, depicted Mrs. Parliament giving birth to
   'a monstrous child, Reformation'.

King. 10	ladies being the most serious article in the sacred oath you took as Patron of the Order of St. George. If he be not able to alembic a receiver fit to be used in the chemistry of generation, he is not capable of marriage, no more than a man is of an estate that wants brains to manage it. Only, I wonder that nothing should
15	content your affections but a blown commodity, which, if not stained, cannot but be ruffled and worsted in the world's opinion, by handling. Neither do I fancy her so accurate[1] a creature as a number of those have lain under
20	your neglect.
Somerset. 25	Were you not my Maker no less than my King, and so numbered among the gods, I should charge you with blasphemy in voting any comparable to her whom Cupid owns for his mother, proclaiming all other beauties idols and herself a true Venus.
King.	If this match will do it, I shall render you as happy as great, resolving to countenance all those [who] opine in favor of the divorce.
Somerset. 30 35	Sire, I have only this to add: that since this feminine love hath not rebated any desire in me to satisfy yours, my enemies might not be gratified with a hope of making your favor[s] so much shine upon Villiers, as wholly to eclipse them towards me.
King. 40	By G--, Villiers is no more to me than the dry bones of my grandfather. 'Tis thou alone, dear Ganymede (<u>the King embraceth and kisseth Somerset</u>), shall quench the thirst of my --
Somerset.	I am assured.

---

1. <u>accurate</u>: finely-made, executed with care (from the Latin sense of the word).

V,iv and v   121

King.   Thou mayest, that I will --- (the King makes a
            mouth another way.¹)

                            Exeunt

(V, iv)   Enter Old Kate, Frances and Turner.

Kate.   Turner hath fitted you with a wench to a hair, and,
            if it may be spoken with reverence to your new
            Countess-ship, no less handsome.

Frances.   But is she a virgin ?

Kate.   As entire as Eve was before she waked her husband 5
            or turned costardmonger to the serpent.

Frances.   Whence comes she ?

Turner.   Out of the mountains, I think, where snow is con-
            gealed into crystal, out of which this she-Pygma-
            lion² was created before her maker had informed her
            with so much fire as might inflame her lust or   10
            tempt her curiosity to the touch of [her] own fin-
            gers.   To conclude, she hath no more potency than
            is required to water the grass.

Frances.   Let's in and instruct her how she shall be managed.
                                                               15
                            Exeunt Omnes.

(V, v)   Enter Overbury, and the Lieutenant of the Tower
            meeting him.

Lieutenant. The errand I come upon suits so untowardly with
            the love and obligations I bear your person that I
            had refused it to the hazard of my office, but that
            I found others as ready to offer performance in
            malice as I was backward out of affection and grati-
            tude--proposing³your going to prison might be by   5

---
1. makes a mouth another way: indicating that he has been
   dissembling all along. See Introduction, p.xxx.
2. she-Pygmalion: O. is confusing the name of the sculptor
   and that of his statue, to which the virgin is compared
   because of her 'unnatural' chastity.
3. proposing: the subject is 'others'.

land, and on foot through the City, in which
you had so often appeared in his Majesty's
or your Lord's coach.

Overbury. Your present employment did the last night
arrive at me, with a copy of the warrant
signed by the enemies of Somerset that procured it--whose eyes[1] (God knows) are too
purblind to see the bottom of the design,
laid only to catch him by his calf Winwood,
whom he licked into a greater proportion of
wealth and honor than was suitable to his
father's birth or his own wit and honesty:
who rewarded the wagon better that carried
him to London than the Carr that brought
him to court and loaded him with all his
preferments.

Lieutenant. The Earl of Somerset seems so strong on
your behalf that he did not only [lay]
upon me his unnecessary command to use all
means for the taking away the tediousness
of your imprisonment, but vowed a sudden
revenge on the authors of your restraint.

Overbury He is a court popingay,[2] and hath learned
to speak what he means no more than he
understands, crying for a rope and an al-
mond with one and the same breath; yet I
wonder how the pied peacock dares thus remove me only to make room for his tail, who
have his life in my hands and, if too much
heated, cannot but melt him into his first
principles he carried under a blue bonnet.
Neither will it sound so much to the honor
of the King--that covers his own fears,
and satisfies the malice of others, out of
an advantage drawn from this young man's
lust.

---

1. eyes: 'Somerset was near-sighted' (O).
2. popingay: parrot.

V,vi

Lieutenant.	Lose not your friends in the crowd of suspicions your perplexed imagination hath mustered up, but rather encourage them for your rescue by a confidence proclaimed to all the world, it being dishonorable to man and unusual with God to suffer the destruction of any that trust them with their preservation.	45
Overbury.	Sir, you know my endeavors were present at your advancement to this place, which gives me this boldness to conjure you that I may not receive by your permission any illegal prejudice.	50
Lieutenant.	If you do, let the Tower be the prospect of my ruin.	55
Overbury.	After some few papers are removed out of the way, I shall wait upon you.	

Exeunt.

(V,vi) *Enter Bess Swallow, Nan To -, and to them Tom Tankard [the Butler], ancient servants to the family and their allies.*

Bess.   How did the Lady Frances behave herself in the hands of the bawdy searchers?

Nan.   She lay flat upon her back like a tumble-stone[1] with her face covered. Where, after the Knight had laid her evidence bare, he spent some time in discoursing of the largeness of the margent, but, when he came to take measure of the diameter, which he did with his pick-tooth, he found it not to exceed that of a small thimble. The same was averred by the rest, who with one vote, like a packed committee, concluded her free from any masculine conjunction whatsoever.   5

                                                                                            10

---

1. **tumble-stone**: the OED defines 'tumbling-stone'as 'a loose stone embedded in clay; a boulder', but I suspect that O. is using the term only for the sake of the sexual pun.

124   V,vi

Nan   There was nothing to be perceived through the door
15   for their block-heads that lay huddled together
              like bowls in a gutter or the nut-headed auditory
              of a tub-preacher; neither could I hold from laugh-
              ing when I saw the nose of the ass, the midwife,
              saddled with spectacles, as if she had been to read
20   a piece of the great Albertus in a Geneva print.[1]

Bess.   'Tis not far short of a miracle that she[2] should
              endure to her age the barking of her bowels, which
              roared so loud in me at fifteen that I was fain to
25   let the nimble barber operate at midnight. Who
              left more behind than he drew out, for which the
              creaking garret[3] would needs question him, though
              all George got by his vaporing was a frotting with
              a cudgel by the mad shaver.

Nan.   Mine _____ carried from my birth no proportion with
30   such an obstruction, yet was thought fit to be
              fomented by Dr. Lister, which made my Lord and I
              travail both in a year. But if I had not found a
              more honorable father, I might have missed of so
              worshipful a husband.

Butler.   You shall ne'er want tents and sop,[4] wenches, to
35   strengthen your backs, if you will communicate this
              new trick of spooning vessels formerly cooled with
              often tasting.   'Twould save me many a gallon in

---

1. the great Albertus in a Geneva print: Albertus Magnus, in
   the small print used for the marginal notes of the English
   translation of the Bible, printed at Geneva in 1560.
2. she: Frances.
3. creaking garret: O. marked a note here, but did not write
   one. This passage, like much of the scene, is extremely
   obscure and probably has some topical reference. 'Garret'
   may refer to George Garrard (see Appendix), but I cannot
   identify the 'barber'. A 'mad shaver' was slang for a
   wild ruffian.
4. tents and sop: 'Sop usually meant a piece of bread soaked
   in liquid, but here it seems to be used in the same sense
   as 'tent', a thickly rolled cloth bandage. The image is
   that of 'leaky' women who need to be 'staunched' or made
   tight (see below, 11.43-5), at least in reputation.

V,vi   125

                    the year, the French pipes[1] being so
                    leaky that they contaminate and farther
                    all they touch.   40

Bess.   We would give money for such a recipe our-
                    selves, that might render us more tight in
                    our husbands' opinions--

Butler.   When you can catch 'em. But had I lain so
                    long at the bung-___[2] as Essex did, I   45
                    should have been perfect in her contents
                    without putting a Secretary of State to
                    the trouble of deciphering it.

                    *A great shout of joy within, and Mrs.Turner
                    coming out.*

Turner.   Are you not mad to gossip here, when
                    nothing is in order, and the King is at   50
                    the gate? --ready to vindicate my lady
                    Frances from all aspersions in relation
                    to honor and womanhood, the court being
                    no less satisfied with her integrity than
                    the defect of Essex.   55

They all cry: We are glad.

                    And so run all out, leaving Turner alone.

Turner.   For I cannot but applaud my invention,
                    that hath been Mother, Nurse, and Mid-
                    wife to such a plot as cannot but render
                    the house of Suffolk great. And, if   60
                    they prove ungrateful, may the spirit of
                    misfortune, that hunted their ancestors,
                    dog them to their graves.
                    Exit.

---

1. *French pipes*: pipes were large vats of wine; 'French' probably alludes to the French disease, or pox. The Butler
   compares the improbable result of the Scrutiny with the
   trick of passing off food and drink as untouched when in
   fact the servants have been at it themselves.
2. *bung-*   : blank in original; obviously, 'bung-hole',
   continuing the metaphor from drinking.

(V, vii)   Enter the King, with Bishops, Doctors, Somerset,
           the Lady Frances, her Father, Sister, and other
           Lords and Retinue.

King.   From that happy throne which, since my assump-
           tion to it, hath been leagued with Peace, Jus-
           tice, and Plenty, I charge you all,[1] especially
           those of the long robe, to tell me if a marriage
5   can be consummated without a man, or where re-
           side such apparent defects as are manifestly
           proved in Essex. For, though divines foist
           in other causes to illustrate no less than make
           necessary the use of their calling in this, as
10   all things else they are able to drag within
           the confines of the Church, yet the principal
           errand of Nature when she sends men and women
           together is generation; and he that cannot
           act this (the only comical scene in this tedious
15   convention) ought in my judgment to be hissed
           off the stage, and another suffered to enter
           that can play the part of a husband. Which I
           speak to discharge my own conscience, not to
           suborn or forestall yours, if any be so mad
20   as to believe the contrary.

All.   We are of your Majesty's opinion, as suiting
           with Law and Reason.

King.   Then I pronounce the Lady Frances not only
           a prodigy in relation to chastity, but free
25   to bestow herself and her beauty where she
           pleases.

Frances.   Being once again restored to my choice by
           your Majesty's justice, I beg leave to cast
           myself at the feet of this noble lord, whom
30   Nature and Fortune hath made me too poor to
           requite.

Somerset. If you will be mine, I shall value you higher
           than a constellation.

Frances.   I am below your acceptance. Yet if you please
35   to take me into your heart, I shall be situated
           more to my content than in the bosom of the
           greatest monarch.

---

1. *I charge you all:* repeated in MS, probably by accident.

V,vii

Enter to them the Duke of Lennox and Countess of Hertford.

Lennox. I humbly desire to be estated with your consent
in this palace, made mine by the Earl of Hertford.

King. I shall proclaim my approbation of your nuptials, 40
to begin the next after Somerset's,[1]

> Whose joys here end, or our diviners lie,
> That say the next will prove a tragedy.

Exeunt

EPILOGUE[2]

You that are wiser, we desire to fence
Our candid Author from the impudence
Of buzzing critics, who like flies do sit
Blowing their spurious censures upon wit,
And fail us actors from their paws that say
Our carriage hath detracted from the play:
A fault beyond our powers to vindicate,
Without their spirits whom we personate.
Yet, could our acting reach the writer's peg,
We'd claim applause--which now we humbly beg.

---

1. next after Somerset's: see Introduction, p.xxxii.

2. Epilogue: Like the prologue, this has reference to an imaginary performance, for which the actors make the conventional apologies. 'You that are wiser' may be meant to follow on from James's final couplet, but it is more likely to be a comparison, in the Jonsonian vein, between the more enlightened members of the audience and the ignorant critics--'flies' to the disdainful author, beasts of prey to the more vulnerable actors. Fail may be a mistake for 'foil', a term used in hunting when the victim managed to deceive the pursuer.

APPENDIX: A Biographical Dictionary of Characters Appearing or Mentioned in Osborne's Text. Capital letters in biography indicate a cross-reference.

ANNE of Denmark, Queen of England (1574-1619). Married to JAMES VI of Scotland (as he was then) in 1589. He made the dangerous voyage across the North Sea to claim his bride, taking the opportunity to visit Tycho Brahe's observatory at the same time. The marriage was not unhappy, though Anne is thought to have had strong sympathies with Catholicism and none at all with her husband's intellectual interests. She is said to have had little influence over him, but her fondness for masques and dancing affected the character of the Jacobean court. James always liked to think that she approved of his favorites. Both for this reason, and because she and the Archbishop of Canterbury (George Abbott) genuinely wanted to find a rival to Somerset, VILLIERS was first introduced into the court under her protection; it was in her bedchamber that he was knighted, on St. George's day, 1615.

ARMSTRONG, Archy (d.1672). Attached at an early age to James VI, he accompanied him to England and became official court jester. He was notoriously rough and rude. In his Traditional Memoirs of King James Osborne tells of his stirring up the King's jealousy against Prince Henry and being tossed in a blanket by the Prince's friends: 'I confesse I did my selfe question Archy long after about it, but he talked though in the affirmative so loud and wildly that I was affraid to waken the attentions of the standers by.' (para.38). But the King treated him well and he was given one of the coveted patents (for making tobacco pipes) in 1618. He accompanied Prince Charles and Buckingham to Spain in 1623 and managed to get into high favor at the Spanish court. He disliked and frequently ridiculed Archbishop Laud. In return, the Archbishop got him discharged from the King's service and the court in 1637, and he was nearly called before Star Chamber. He lived to gloat over Laud's imprisonment, and had accumulated enough wealth to end his life in a comfortable retirement.

BEDFORD, Lady: See Lucy HARRINGTON

BLOUNT, Charles, Earl of Mountjoy and Earl of Devonshire (1563-1606). Succeeded his friend Essex as Commander in Chief in Ireland, and won a decisive victory over the rebels and their Spanish allies (at Kinsale, in 1601). On his return to England in 1603 he was created Earl of Devonshire. He had been a lover of Essex's sister, Lady Penelope RICH for many years, and finally married her after her divorce in 1605. Laud, who was Mountjoy's chaplain at the time, performed the ceremony.

BOOKER, John (1603-1667). His reputation was second only to LILLY's and indeed stood higher before Lilly appeared on the scene, because he made a number of accurate predictions in his first almanac of 1631. He and Lilly were both attacked by the Royalist astrologer Sir George Wharton. The Dutch Fortune-Teller, which is rather enigmatically mentioned in I,iii, is now thought to be spurious. It is a set of codes in the form of wheels which indicate a way of looking up an answer to one's questions - mostly either financial or matrimonial.

BRUCE, Edward, Lord Kinloss and Baron Bruce of Kinless(1549?-1611). Scots judge and diplomat. Thought to have arranged the secret correspondence between JAMES and Robert CECIL which helped to secure James's accession to the English throne. He accompanied the King to England and received his peerage, with many other honors, soon thereafter. According to Bishop Burnet, it was for this reason that successful Scots were called Sons of Bruce. (History of His Own Time, 6 vols, 6th ed., Oxford 1823 [rep. Hildesheim, 1969], I, p.15).

BRYDGES, Frances, Countess of Exeter (1580-1663). A daughter of the Earl of Chandos, who was first married to Sir Thomas Smith, Master of Requests, then to the Earl of Exeter, Thomas Cecil, who was nearly forty years her senior. She was converted to Catholicism, supposedly by Tobie MATHEW. In 1619 she was the victim of a series of accusations by her granddaughter-in-law, the wife of Lord Roos; these included incest and attempted murder. A Star Chamber hearing completely exonerated her. See also LAKE; William CECIL, Lord Roos; and Introduction, pp.xxii-xxiii.

BUCKINGHAM: See VILLIERS.

Appendix

CAESAR, Madam. Possibly the wife of Sir Julius Caesar (1558-1636), who was one of the commissioners for the Essex divorce in 1613, and also Chancellor of the Exchequer and Master of the Rolls. Osborne might also be thinking of the wife of Sir Julius's son Charles (1590-1642), who was a daughter of the rich jewel merchant, Sir Peter Vanlore. Given his attitude to citizens, he might well have regarded a woman from such a background as little better than a bawd.

CAMPDEN, Viscount: See Baptist HICKS.

CARLISLE, Lord: See James HAY

CARR, or Ker, Robert, Earl of Somerset (c.1590-1645). After first attracting the King's attention when he broke his leg at a tilt in 1607 (James is said to have taught him Latin during his convalescence), this handsome young man went on to become the most notorious of the Scottish favorites. Osborne's description of him (p. 6), may be compared with that of Arthur Wilson (History of Great Britain, p.83): 'For his Person, He was rather well compacted than tall; his feature and favor comely, and handsome, than beautiful; the hair of his head flaxen, that of his face tinctured with yellow, of the Sycambrian color. In his own nature, of a gentle mind, and affable disposition, having publick affections, till they were all swallowed up in this gulf of beauty, which did precipitate him into these dangerous Contrivances.' For his subsequent career, see Introduction, pp. xx-xxiii.

CECIL, Robert, Earl of Salisbury (1563?-1612). Son of William Cecil, Lord Burghley (1520-1598), Queen Elizabeth's chief minister of state. His own fortunes began to rise only after the accession of James I, with whom he conducted a secret correspondence during the last years of the Queen's reign; it was largely thanks to his diplomacy that the English Privy Council accepted the new ruler with so little argument. He became Lord Treasurer in 1608. Though he received a pension from Spain and made substantial profits out of his government posts, he seems generally to have been regarded as a relatively honest, though never popular, statesman. Clarendon describes his son, William Cecil (Lord Cranborne, in the play), as having inherited the title, but not the virtues, of his famous father.

CECIL, William, Lord Roos, or Ross (1590-1618). Grandson to Thomas Cecil, Earl of Exeter, who was brother to Robert Cecil. He first travelled abroad in 1605 and remained out of the country for three years; in 1612 he visited Italy, and in 1616, as ambassador to Spain, was abroad again for a year. Before his departure he married Anne, daughter of Sir Thomas Lake. For what followed, see Introduction, pp. xxii-xxiii. His servant Diego, mentioned by Osborne, was urged by Lady Exeter to come back to England to testify in the lawsuit of 1619, but, according to Chamberlain, he was warned by GONDOMAR and went off to Spain instead.

CHAPMAN, George (1559?-1634). Poet, playwright, and translator. Robert CARR was his patron; he dedicated his translation of the Odyssey to him in 1614 and composed an allegorical poem on the Perseus and Andromeda story to celebrate the wedding in 1613. He later had to defend himself from criticism of his choice of subject matter. But he remained loyal to Somerset, dedicating a poem to him as late as 1622. Most of his writing for the stage was, as Osborne says, the result of poverty. It helped him to finance his greatest work, the complete translation of Homer.

COKE, Sir Edward, Lord Chief Justice (1551-1634). Coke began as a protege of Lord Burghley's and rose rapidly. He was involved in the prosecution of most of the eminent figures who came to trial in this period: Essex and Southampton in 1601, RALEGH in 1603, the gunpowder plotters in 1605, and the Somersets in 1615-16. His violence and rudeness on the bench were notorious. In June 1616 he was suspended and later removed from the Bench; it was at this time that the letter printed in the Cabala first appeared, attributed to Bacon, though now thought not to be his. He was married (1598) to Lady Elizabeth Hatton, with whom he had many quarrels, first over property and then over the marriage of their daughter to one of Buckingham's relations. He came back to public life in the 1620s and became a leader of the popular side in Parliament, attacking monopolies and the proposed Spanish marriage. His last great speech in the Commons was an attack on Buckingham. By the King's orders, his papers were seized immediately after his death (cf. what Osborne says about Salisbury on p.12).

CON or CONN, George (d. 1640). A Scot by birth, he was brought up a Catholic and educated at various seminaries abroad. He was a Dominican, not a Jesuit. As Papal agent to Henrietta Maria, from 1636-39, he made his house in Long

Acre a centre for the Catholic gentry and new converts.

CRANBORNE, Lady: See Catherine HOWARD.

CRANFIELD, Lionel, Earl of Middlesex (1575-1645). He began as an apprentice, married his master's daughter, rose to become a Merchant Adventurer and, through the Earl of NORTHAMPTON's recommendation, was brought into the King's service. From 1613 on, he held many court posts and made many much-needed reforms in them. He helped bring down both Suffolk and Bacon, and became Lord Treasurer in 1622. But, despite his marriage to a relation of Buckingham's, he made an enemy of the favorite, who joined with others to impeach him in 1624; he lost all his offices and was imprisoned briefly, after which he lived mainly in retirement. He tried to remain neutral in the Civil War, but his son took the side of Parliament.

DERBY ('great Derby'). Hertford's remark (III, iv, 8-12) could refer to any of the Stanley family who held that title; I have found no reference to anyone who disguised himself as a juggler. But James, the 7th Earl (1607-1651), was one of several Derbys who patronised a company of players and Peter du MOULIN, whom Osborne probably knew, was his chaplain.

DEVEREUX, Robert, 3rd Earl of Essex (1591-1646). Son of Queen Elizabeth's favorite, the second Earl of Essex (1567-1601), who was executed for his abortive uprising against her. By Act of Parliament, he was restored to his father's title in 1604. JAMES I also arranged the marriage between him and FRANCES HOWARD, in an attempt to put an end to the enmity between her family and that of Essex. The young Earl went on his travels in 1607-9. His divorce took place in 1613, after which he kept away from the English court as much as possible. In 1620 he briefly commanded a company in the Palatinate; in 1625 he was Vice Admiral on the Cadiz expedition. By now he was known as a member of the popular party in the Lords. He married a second time in 1631. His wife, Elizabeth Paulet, had one child which died in infancy. She was accused of adultery and they separated. In 1642 he became general of the Parliamentary forces; in 1645, he anticipated the Self-Denying Ordinance by laying down his command. Though he had not been a successful leader, he was a respected figure, and in 1646 he was given a state funeral at public expense.

DENBIGH, Countess of: See VILLIERS.

DIGBY, John, 1st Earl of Bristol (1580-1653). Attracting the King's favor early in the new reign, he rose rapidly over the heads of many senior diplomats to become ambassador to Spain in 1611. While there, he learned, and informed JAMES, of the secret Spanish pensions received by many of his most trusted advisers, including SALISBURY. Though he had advised against a Spanish marriage for Prince Henry, he was later involved in negotiations on behalf of Prince Charles: in 1614, in 1617-18, and finally in 1622-23, when Charles and Buckingham unexpectedly arrived in Spain. The breakdown of the negotiations led to a quarrel between them and the ambassador, and when Charles succeeded to the throne Digby was in disgrace. He later took the King's side in the Civil War, and was one of the royalists most hated by Parliament. His unpopularity on both sides was probably the result of his long residence in Spain - as Chamberlain comments in 1617, he 'speaks too much Spanish' (Letters, II, p.64) - and to the suspicion that he was a Roman Catholic.

ELIZABETH, Princess (Elizabeth of Bohemia) (1596-1662). Came to court only in 1608, and left England a few months after her marriage in February 1613. She and her large family were soon caught up in the war which followed on the Palsgrave's decision to accept the crown of Bohemia; many Englishmen, especially the more committed Protestants, felt that James ought to have taken a more active part on behalf of his daughter and son-in-law, but he did allow some troops to be raised to fight in Germany. After her husband's death in 1632 she lived mainly on the Continent, in poverty, returning to England only after the Restoration. Two of her sons fought for Charles I during the Civil War.

ESSEX, Earl of: See Robert DEVEREUX.

EXETER: See Frances BRYDGES, Countess of Exeter.

FENTON, Joseph. A colleague of Dr. William Harvey at St. Bartholomew's Hospital, in Smithfield.

FORMAN, Simon (1552-1611). He began his career in Wiltshire, the county of his birth, and probably had some contact with the Hertford and Pembroke families then. He came to London in 1589 and commenced a highly successful career as astrologer and magician. Among those who consulted him were many court ladies, including Frances HOWARD (2), who asked in 1597 about her chances of marrying the Earl of Southampton. The Earl of HERTFORD also asked his advice. Frances HOWARD (1), like many of his clients, became excessively dependent on him. During the murder trial of the Somersets in 1615-16, her letters to him were read out in court, and much interest was aroused in the display of various images, which he was said to have given her as a means of making her husband impotent.

FORTESCUE, Sir John (1531?-1607). Chancellor of the Exchequer from 1589, and by the end of Elizabeth's reign holder of many other offices as well. He kept these posts after James's accession but lost the Chancellorship, supposedly because he tried to persuade the other Privy Councillors to offer James VI the crown of England only on certain conditions.

FREDERICK, Elector Palatine (1596-1632). The 'Palsgrave', as he was often called in England, was one of the six Electors who, besides ruling separate kingdoms of Germany, had the right to elect the Emperor of the Holy Roman Empire; he ruled the Palatinate, with its capital at Heidelberg. He married James I's daughter Elizabeth in 1613. His decision in 1619 to accept the crown of Bohemia, when the Protestants of that country deposed their Catholic ruler, was the immediate cause of the Thirty Years' War, in which his own part was consistently disastrous. It is with hindsight that Osborne refers to him in the play; at the time of his marriage, he was extremely popular with English Protestants.

GAGE, George (b.after 1582, d.c. 1640). A Roman Catholic political agent, who was apparently ordained along with Sir Tobie MATHEW in Rome in 1614. He was used by James I as an agent at the papal court in 1621, when he was seeking a dispensation for Charles's marriage to the Spanish Infanta, a project which came to nothing. In the 1640s he was sent to prison, and seems to have died there.

GARRARD, or Garrett, George (1580? - ?). A well-known wit and letter-writer, mentioned by Thomas Coryate in Coryate's Crudities (1611) as a member of the 'Mermaid Club'. He may be the 'creaking garret' referred to in V, vi, in which case this mysterious passage might refer to some now-forgotten practical joke.

GLOVER, Sir Thomas (d.1625). He served as Ambassador to Constantinople in 1605, English agent in Turkey in 1611, and co-ambassador there in 1619. When he suddenly died in 1625, according to Chamberlain, he 'was so poore that the Turkie companie was faine to be at charge to burie him' (<u>Letters</u>, II, p.615).

GONDOMAR: Don Diego Sarmiento de Acuna
He first came to England as ambassador in 1613 and soon established a great ascendancy over James. His insistence that Ralegh should be punished for his attack on Spanish possessions on his unsuccessful voyage of 1616-17 was one of the major factors that led James to order his execution. Gondomar's first term as ambassador ended in 1618, but he returned for a second term from 1620 to 1622. In 1624 he was satirized as the Black Knight in Middleton's <u>Game at Chess,</u> which attacked the Spanish faction and the proposed Spanish marriage.

GORING, George, Earl of Norwich (1583-1663). He was a well-known courtier and wit under both James I and Charles I, and Weldon describes him as one of the King's 'chief and master fools'. In the Civil War he fought on the royalist side, was sentenced to death after the surrender of Colchester in 1648, but pardoned; later he joined Charles II on the Continent, and returned with him in 1660. Osborne may also have been recalling his son, George Goring, Baron Goring (1608-1657), a profligate courtier who betrayed the royalist Army Plot of 1641 to Parliament in order to save himself, but finally declared himself for the King, fought on the royalist side, and died in poverty in Madrid.

HADDINGTON, Lady: See Elizabeth RADCLIFFE.

HAMILTON, James, 2nd Marquis Hamilton (1589-1625). A faithful servant of King James, though an opponent of his pro-Spanish policies. Osborne's praise of his merciful behavior in Star Chamber seems justified: he mitigated the sentence against Bacon in 1621 and spoke against Buckingham's attempt to imprison DIGBY in 1624. His friend and physician George Eglisham insisted that his death was the result of poisoning by the Buckingham family, a charge which was resurrected on several occasions. Osborne may also be thinking (especially in III,iv) of his son, James, 3rd Marquis, later Duke, of Hamilton (1606-1649). The latter was a favorite of Charles I, but his influence and advice were disastrous. He was accused in 1631 of plotting, while in Scotland, to seize the throne for himself· (he was the next heir to it after the reigning family), and his enemies thought that the same motive inspired him during the war, when he often seemed to be playing one side off against the other. He was executed shortly after Charles I. His marriage

Appendix

which Osborne mentions on p.31 took place when he was thirteen and his wife, Buckingham's niece, was only seven.

HARINGTON, Lucy, Countess of Bedford (1581-1627). Because she was a patroness and friend of poets--including Donne, Jonson, and Daniel--the Countess of Bedford attracted much praise from her contemporaries. She was a favorite of Queen Anne's, and one of the liveliest participants at court masques and festivities in the early years of the reign. But serious illness and her family's financial difficulties clouded her later years and made her one of the greediest seekers of monopolies as a solution to her debts. It is this side of her character, presumably, that explains Osborne's unsympathetic reference to her in IV,i.

HAY, James, 1st Earl of Carlisle (d.1636). One of the first, and longest-lived, of the Scots favorites from James's early years in England. As Frances's remark in II, i, shows, he had a reputation for extravagance; Osborne comments in the Traditional Memoirs on his invention of the 'Ante-Supper', in which a vast banquet was set out for show only and then, when the guests had looked their fill, 'in a manner throwne away, and fresh set on to the same height, having only this advantage of the other, that it was hot.' (para. 39). The King used him on many diplomatic missions. In 1617 he married Lucy Percy (1599-1660). She was daughter to the imprisoned Earl of NORTHUMBERLAND, who had been much averse to the match and kept her with him in the Tower for a time. She went on to become the closest friend of Henrietta Maria, and the most popular figure at the Caroline court, though after the execution of her friend Strafford she switched her allegiance for a time; it was she who betrayed to Parliament Charles I's intention of arresting the five members, and during the war she was involved in numerous intrigues.

HELWYS, or Elwys, Sir Gervase (1561-1615). Appointed Lieutenant of the Tower in 1613, in place of Sir William Waad (or Wade), who had proved inconveniently scrupulous in obeying the orders that no one was to have access to OVERBURY during his imprisonment. He had to pay the Howards £2000 for the post, and he also agreed, at least tacitly, to act in their interest. He had been a fellow-student of Overbury, at the Middle Temple, and seems to have been horrified when he first learned that some of the food sent him from the Countess of Essex was poisoned. He was too frightened to report what he knew, and contented himself, according to his testimony later, with trying to prevent the poison from reaching his prisoner. When the scandal came to light, he was put on trial and executed, at his own request, not at Tyburn but on Tower Hill (hence his final speech in V,ii). His estate was granted to William Earl of PEMBROKE, who was considered very generous because he returned it to the widow and her children.

HENRY, Prince of Wales (1594-1612). Osborne comments in the Traditional Memoirs of King James: 'The palpable partiality that descended from the Father to the Scots, did Estate the whole Love of the English upon his Son Henry: whom they ingaged by so much expectation, as it may be doubted, whether it ever lay in the power of any prince meerly humane, to bring so much felicity into a Nation, as they did all his Life propose to themselves at the Death of King James.' (para.37). The Prince was a friend of Ralegh, took an interest in the martial arts which his father disliked, and was a staunch Protestant, known to be opposed to the proposed Spanish marriage for himself. Some historians of the 1650s also suggest that he had been Frances HOWARD'S first lover, or that he had been a rival of CARR, or that he knew of their love affair and spoke scoffingly of it. Naturally, many attributed his death to poison, and found the motive either in Carr's rivalry or the King's fear of his son's popularity.

HERBERT, Philip, Earl of Montgomery and 4th Earl of Pembroke (1584-1650). He was a much less distinguished character than his famous brother William. Many stories are told of the quarrels in which his hot temper involved him, but he kept the King's favor, according to Osborne, better than his brother. Nevertheless, he belonged to the popular party, sided with Parliament, and sat in the Commons after the House of Lords was abolished in 1649. As a former Lord Chamberlain and Chancellor of Oxford, he might have been expected to take a lenient attitude both to the stage and to the royalist leanings of that University. Instead, he was opposed to the resumption of public performances, and presided over the Visitation of Oxford, when Episcopalian scholars and fellows were turned out of their places. Hence, he became a favorite target for royalist attacks.

HERBERT, William, 3rd Earl of Pembroke 1580-1630).Osborne lived in his household for a time, so what he says about him is probably based on observation. The remark in III,i, suggests what is confirmed elsewhere, that he had a reputation for sexual license (he was imprisoned in 1600 for

Appendix   139

getting Mary Fitton with child). In 1604 he married Mary
Talbot, daughter of the Earl of Shrewsbury, on whom Clarendon comments: 'He paid much too dear for his wife's fortunes by taking her person into the bargain'. He succeeded
Somerset as Lord Chamberlain, and held the office until 1626.
His political views were pro-Protestant and anti-Spanish. He
came increasingly to support the popular party against the
court, though he never played an important political role:
hence, perhaps, Osborne's suggestion that someone had a hold
over him (See Introduction, p.iii).

HERTFORD, Earl of: see Edward SEYMOUR. Countess of: see
Frances HOWARD (2).

HICKS, Sir Baptist, 1st Viscount Campden (1551-1629). The
son of a rich mercer, he was brought up in his father's
business, a fact which Jacobean snobs never let him forget.
Although he received a knighthood shortly after James's
accession, and became immensely rich, he continued to keep a
shop.   Chamberlain comments in 1618 on the strangeness of
seeing Bacon, in his robes of the Council, go to Hicks's
shop 'to cheapen and buy silkes and velvets'. (Letters, II,
p.157).

HOBART, Sir Henry   (d. 1625). He became Lord Chief
Justice of Common Pleas in 1613, and was involved in
Suffolk's trial for corruption (at which he spoke against
the harshness of the original fine) and in the examination
of Lady Roos.

HOWARD, Catherine, Lady Cranbourne, later Lady Salisbury.
She was married to William Cecil, the only son of Robert
CECIL, in 1608, when they were both very young. Her first
child was born in 1613 , a fact which may give some point to
Frances's remarks in I, iv.

HOWARD, Charles, Lord Howard of Effingham and Earl of
Nottingham (1536-1624), Lord High Admiral. He was a prominent figure at Elizabeth's court, and commanded against
Spain in 1587, also, jointly with Essex, in 1596. It was
to him that the Queen named James as her successor. James
continued to favor him, though his embassy to Spain in 1604
provoked the scornful remark of the fool STONE, for which
the Admiral had him whipped. The best gloss on some of the
allusions to him in TT is Osborne's comment in Traditional
Memoirs of Queen Elizabeth: 'Neither was there a goodlier
man for person in Europe, as my eyes did witness though they
met not with him before he was turned towards the point of

80, no youth being more celebrated for gallantry and good fortune than his. I confess that in his age he married a young lady allied to King James, which set his wisdom many degrees back in the repute of the world' (para 173, p.65). Those who made fun of the old man for this exploit included the drunken King Christian of Denmark, who made horns at him. (See G.P.V. Akrigg, Jacobean Pageant, pp.80-81.)

HOWARD, Elizabeth, Lady Wallingford (1586-1658). Shortly before her sister Frances, she made an arranged marriage which was nearly as disastrous in its results. In 1605, she was nineteen and her husband, Baron William KNOLLYS, was fifty-six. The only surviving children of this marriage were born in 1627 and 1631--one of them at the house of Edward Lord Vaux, whom she married in 1632, five weeks after her husband's death. In 1641 a complicated paternity suit began; for the next 150 years, these two children and their descendants tried to establish their claim as heirs to Knollys's title, Earl of Banbury. But the House of Lords could not be persuaded to believe them.

HOWARD, Frances (1), Countess of Essex, then Countess of Somerset (1590-1632). See Introduction, pp. xx-xxii, for the earlier part of her career. Within two years of her marriage to Somerset, the charge of murder was raised. Her only child, a daughter, was born during the period when she was awaiting her trial. When she was brought to the Tower, she pleaded not to be lodged in OVERBURY'S rooms and was given instead the ones that had formerly been occupied by Ralegh (he had just been released in order to make his voyage to South America). At the trial her letters provided evidence that she had been suspiciously concerned with Overbury's diet and that she had certainly intended to poison him, whether or not she had directly caused his death. She pleaded guilty, but was pardoned in July 1616, though she remained in the Tower until 1622. A number of writers say that she and Somerset never got on well after this, and also insinuate that she died of venereal disease, but these reports may well be inspired by the desire to find a moral to the story. Her daughter Anne married the Earl of Bedford; their son was the republican Lord William Russell, executed in 1683 for the Rye House Plot.

HOWARD, Frances (2), Countess of Hertford, then Duchess of Lennox and Richmond (1578-1639). A cousin of the more notorious Frances Howard; her father, Thomas Howard, Viscount

Appendix

Bindon, was brother to the Earl of Surrey who was Suffolk's grandfather. Her first marriage, to the rich wine merchant Pranell, was seen as a mésalliance, and after his early death she looked around for a suitably noble husband to make up for it. In 1597 she consulted FORMAN about her chances of marrying the worthy Earl of Southampton, but she settled for HERTFORD, nearly forty years her senior, in 1600. (An unsuccessful suitor, Sir George Rodney, is said to have committed suicide in despair.) Hertford's claim to the English crown, which had led Elizabeth I to imprison him during much of his youth, must have been a point in his favor, since, according to Arthur Wilson, she was notoriously proud: 'She would often discourse of her two Grand-Fathers, the Dukes of Norfolk and Buckingham; recounting the time since one of her Grand-Fathers did this, the other did that: But if the Earl her Husband came in presence, she would quickly desist; for when he found her in those Exaltations, to take her down, he would say, Frank, Frank, How long is it since thou wert Married to Prannel? which would damp the Wings of her Spirit, and make her look after her feet, aswell [sic] as gawdy Plumes.' (History, p.258). Hertford kept her as much as possible on one or the other of his Wiltshire estates, but, according to Wilson, LENNOX managed to see her in disguise. She finally married him within a month of Hertford's death in 1621. Lennox was granted his second Dukedom of Richmond (the first was a Scottish title) at the same time that Buckingham was made a Duke. His wife's enemies now called her the 'double-duchess' (Chamberlain, Letters, II, p.499). Wilson claims that after Lennox's death in 1624, she had hopes of ensnaring the widowed James I, the only partner in the kingdom she now considered worthy of her (History, p.257). She seems to have been financially rapacious as well as proud (some shady transactions are recorded in Menna Prestwich, Cranfield, Politics and Profits under the Early Stuarts, Oxford 1966, pp.412-20). The Pedlar's remark about orris hangings in III, i,94-7 may be less random than it seems. The Mortlake tapestry works, the first in England, were started by Sir Frances Crane in 1619; Osborne may have remembered either that Crane and the Duchess had a joint patent for coinage of farthing tokens, or that her row with Lionel CRANFIELD, who bought Copt Hall from her, involved the question of whether the wall hangings had been included in the purchase price. The Duchess and Lennox are buried in Westminster Abbey, where she raised an enormous monument to them both.

HOWARD, Henry, Earl of Northampton (1540-1614). Few historians have a good word for this man, whose career was based on intrigue and flattery. Some explanation may perhaps be found in his background. His father, the poet Surrey, was beheaded for treason in 1547. He was brought up, depending on who was on the throne, first as a Protestant, then a Catholic, then a Protestant. His older brother, Thomas Duke of Norfolk, was beheaded in 1572 for intriguing on behalf of Mary Queen of Scots, and he himself was suspected of involvement in the plot. He was imprisoned several times during Elizabeth's reign. Not surprisingly, he saw the Scottish king as his only hope for an escape from the poverty and obscurity in which he lived, and it was he who wrote on CECIL's behalf during the secret correspondence which prepared the way for the new reign. His rewards were great: under James, he received an earldom in 1604, became Lord Privy Seal in 1608, and until his death in 1614 was one of the most powerful men in the kingdom. He was always suspected of being a secret Roman Catholic, even though he publicly spoke against the Gunpowder plotters; Protestants noted that no pro-Catholic pamphleteer attacked him for this, and concluded that he had simply been preserving his cover. He succeeded, however, in persuading the Star Chamber to fine those who circulated such stories about him. At Salisbury's death he was considered the most likely successor for the office of Treasurer; instead, he was made one of a commission which handled treasury affairs until his nephew Suffolk was appointed to the office on 10 June, 1614. Northampton died only five days later, but his resentment was such that he altered his will at the last minute to revoke a bequest to Suffolk. His will also shows him to have died a Roman Catholic. The fact that his body was taken to Dover for burial gave rise to the rumor, which Osborne mentions, that it was transported later to Rome. He had played a great part in Carr's affair with Frances (his great-niece), and some of the letters produced at the Overbury murder trial contained passages which were considered unfit to read out in court. His conduct throughout Overbury's imprisonment had been extremely suspicious; whether or not he had a hand in the murder, he had certainly been hoping that the prisoner would die.

HOWARD, Thomas, 1st Earl of Suffolk (1561-1626). He seems to have been much less clever than his uncle, but better liked and trusted by his contemporaries. Though the son of the Duke of Norfolk, a man executed for treason, he was restored in blood in 1584 and won the favor of Queen Elizabeth, under whom he had a distinguished naval career.

Appendix

James I made him a privy councillor, then a peer, almost as soon as he arrived in England, and Howard's list of honors went on accumulating: Lord Chamberlain until 1614, then Lord High Treasurer. Many of his problems, and those of his daughters, seem to have been due to the influence of his second wife, Katherine KNEVET. In 1618, he was brought before Star Chamber to answer accusations of fraud in the running of the Treasury. He, his wife, and some of his officials, turned out to have been amazingly corrupt even for those days, and were heavily fined and imprisoned. They were never altogether ruined, and in 1621 he was able to get his own back by urging that Bacon be brought to trial, but the Howard family had come to the end of its power.

JAMES VI of Scotland and I of England (1566-1625). The son of Mary Queen of Scots and Henry Stewart, Lord Darnley, though his enemies claimed to be sceptical about the identity of his father. After Mary had been forced to abdicate in 1567 he was crowned King of Scots, and he never saw her after that time. She virtually disinherited him in 1586 by bequeathing her dominions to Philip II of Spain and he made no real attempt to save her from execution, though he did not directly consent to it, as Osborne hints. He married Anne of Denmark in 1589 and she bore him seven children, of whom three survived their infancy. In attributing Prince Henry's death to his father's jealousy Osborne is only echoing a widespread contemporary belief, but his suggestion that the rest were secretly murdered, because James disliked large families (p.61), is more than usually irresponsible. The aspects of James's rule with which the play is chiefly concerned are his desire for a union of England and Scotland (which did not finally happen until 1707), his excessive and embarrassing indulgence to his favorites, the marriage of his daughter to a Protestant ruler whose cause he then failed to support, and his repeated and unsuccessful attempts to marry one of his sons to the Spanish Infanta. Elswhere, Osborne describes him 'in the colors I saw him in the next Progresse after his Inauguration, which was as Greene as the grasse he trod on, with a Feather in his Cap, and a horne instead of a Sword by his side: How suitable to his Age, Calling, or Person, I leave to others to judge from his Pictures.' (Memoirs of King James, para. 17, p.54)

KINGSMILL. It is not clear why Osborne describes this whole family in such harsh terms (IV, i,). The widow of Sir William Kingsmill was the second wife of Edward Lord ZOUCHE. The name Bridget Kingsmill was used as an alias by one of

Forman's clients, Lady Norris, daughter of the Earl of Oxford, in 1598.

KNEVET or KNYVET, Catherine, Countess of Suffolk. As Osborne says, her beauty was famous, at least until she had the smallpox in 1619. She married Thomas HOWARD in 1583 and bore him seven sons and three daughters. Her main concern seems to have been the aggrandisement of her own family. She was at one time thought to be Robert Cecil's mistress, and Osborne carries the insinuation further by suggesting in I,ii, 43-5, that Cecil deliberately married his son to his (perhaps) daughter in the hope of ensuring an heir of his own blood even if she proved unfaithful to her husband. The building of Audley End was her idea, and it was generally said to have been paid for with Spanish gold, because she, unlike her husband, was in the pay of Spain. During his time as Lord Treasurer she took bribes from those who wanted access to him, and drew heavily on the public funds for their private expenses.

KNOLLYS, William, Viscount Wallingford and Earl of Banbury (1547-1632). Though he was dragged into the Howard family intrigues by his marriage with Elizabeth Howard in 1605, he seems to have kept more reputation than most of the others. In 1613 he and the Earl of Southampton represented Essex at the preliminary hearing to discuss the Essex divorce. This might suggest that he was already trying to keep his distance from his wife's family. Though he became Viscount Wallingford in 1616, his career suffered at the time of Suffolk's disgrace; James insisted on his resigning his post as Master of the Court of Wards, saying that 'he had one fault ... which could not stand with his service nor of the state, that he was altogether guided and overruled by an arch-wife' (Chamberlain, Letters, II, 206-7). Charles I, however, favored him and made him Earl of Banbury in 1626. A child born early in the marriage died in infancy; for the others, see Elizabeth HOWARD.

LAKE, Anne, Lady Roos or Ross. The daughter of Sir Thomas Lake, a follower of the Howard family, who became Secretary of State jointly with Sir Ralph Winwood in 1616. At about the same time she was married to the young Lord Roos. For the results, see Introduction, pp. xxii-xxiii.

LENNOX, Duke of: See Lodovick Stuart

LESLIE, Alexander, 1st Earl of Leven (1580?-1661). Essentially a soldier, who spent much of his active life on the Continent - under Vere in the Netherlands, then in Sweden from 1605, where he served under both Charles IX and Gustavus Adolphus. In 1638 he offered to lead an English expedition for the recovery of the Bohemian throne. In 1639 he led the Scots in the first Bishops' War, and captured Aberdeen and Edinburgh. As a conciliatory measure, after peace had been concluded in 1641, Charles I made him an Earl, but he fought for Parliament in the Civil War and in 1644 led a Scots army into England. He had Charles I in his custody in 1645 and tried to persuade him to take the Covenant to establish a Presbyterian church government in England. (The Scots were later accused of selling their King to Cromwell; this is the point of Lennox's line in II, vii,45ff.) Under the Commonwealth, he supported Charles II and was one of the generals of the unsuccessful invasion army; though imprisoned briefly after the defeat at Worcester, he was allowed to spend his last years in Scotland.

LILLY, William (1602-1681). The most famous astrologer of the Civil War. He always claimed to be sympathetic to Charles I and to have tried to assist in his escape from Carisbrooke Castle. But he was generally thought of as pro-Parliament, and his prophecies tended to stress the fall of kings and other disasters. Royalists tended therefore to scoff at him and at astrology.

LISTER, Dr. Matthew (1571?-1656). He and his brother Edward (1556-1620) were among the most famous court physicians of the period. His patients included Robert Cecil, Queen Anne, Charles I, and the dowager Countess of Pembroke (Mary Sidney), who took him with her to the Spa in 1617, giving rise to rumors that she intended to marry him. I do not know whether there is any contemporary scandal lying behind the mysterious obscenities of the servants' dialogue in V, vi, where his name figures.

MANNERS, Roger, 5th Earl of Rutland (1576-1612). Osborne's note about him probably applies to his involvement in two duels, and to the fact that his wife Elizabeth, whom he married in 1599, had no children by him, though she was the object of attentions from other men. According to one story, OVERBURY wrote his <u>Wife</u> as a way of courting her. She died in 1615.

MATTHEW or MATHEW, Sir Tobie (1577-1655). Though his father was Archbishop of York, he himself was converted to Catholicism on a trip to Italy in 1606, by the Jesuit, Robert PARSONS. The Archbishop of Canterbury tried unsuccessfully to reconvert him on his return, by imprisoning him for six months. On his next visit to Italy he enrolled at a seminary and was ordained in 1614. He was a writer and a wit, and a friend of Donne and Bacon (whose essays he translated into Italian in 1618). Though he dressed as a layman, he made many converts among the intelligensia, during his periods of residence in England; these were interspersed with periods of banishment when his successes became too embarrassing. In 1640 the House of Commons petitioned for his banishment, and he spent the rest of his life in exile.

MAYNARD, Sir John (1592-1658). From what little is known of this courtier, it is not clear why Osborne includes him in the category of fools mentioned by Stone in I, ii. Maynard is mentioned in Chamberlain's letters for his dancing, and for a masque (now lost) which he composed in 1623. It is perhaps his inconstancy, in supporting first Buckingham, then Parliament, and then (in 1647) the Presbyterian-Royalist coalition, that made Osborne so scornful of him.

MIDDLESEX, Earl of: See Lionel CRANFIELD.

MOLLE, John (1558?-1638). This scholar, who was distantly related to the Osborne family, became a cause célebre through his imprisonment by the Inquisition in 1608, when he was accompanying Lord ROOS on his travels in Italy. Sir Henry WOTTON and others attempted to procure his release, but he died in captivity thirty years later. A letter of Wotton's, published in the Cabala (1654), hints that Roos had somehow been responsible for the arrest.

MOUNTJOY, see Charles BLOUNT, Earl of Mountjoy.

DR. DU MOULIN. There are three men of this name to whom Osborne could be referring:

1. Pierre du Moulin (1568-1658). A French Protestant divine, he came to England with the famous physician Theodore Turquet de Mayerne in 1615, and eventually settled there. He was a royalist, but his two sons were, at least on the surface, supporters of the Commonwealth. They were:

Appendix

2. Peter du Moulin (1601-1684). An Anglican divine who is most famous for his secret authorship of an answer to Milton's Defensio, but who nevertheless obtained a D.D. at Oxford in 1656, and

3. Lewis du Moulin (1606-1680). An Oxford graduate who probably practised medicine there, and became a professor of Ancient History in place of an ejected royalist.

All three of these could have been among Osborne's acquaintances at Oxford. Lewis du Moulin, like Osborne, wrote a pamphlet advocating the taking of the Engagement to the Commonwealth.

NORTHAMPTON: See Henry HOWARD, Earl of Northampton.

NORTHUMBERLAND: See Henry PERCY, Earl of Northumberland.

O'NEILL, Hugh, 2nd Earl of Tyrone (1540?-1616). Known in England chiefly as the leader of rebellion in Ireland from 1595, when he was first proclaimed traitor. In 1599 Essex was sent to Ireland to put down the rebellion, his failure to do so led, indirectly, to his own execution in 1601. His friend Charles BLOUNT, Earl of Mountjoy, was more successful. That Tyrone received a royal pardon in 1603 angered a number of people as well as Osborne, but it had been offered by Elizabeth rather than James (Tyrone did not know of her death when he accepted it). In 1607 he was summoned to England to answer charges of stirring up a fresh rebellion; in a panic, he fled to the Continent, and spent the rest of his life in Rome, receiving pensions from the Pope and the King of Spain.

OVERBURY, Sir Thomas (1581-1613). After attending Oxford and the Middle Temple, he first met CARR on a journey to Edinburgh; when Carr came to England in 1603 they became close friends, and he clearly believed, as he told Carr in a letter read out at the trial, that 'you owe me for all the fortune, wit, and understanding that you have'. As Carr rose at the court, so did Overbury. His insolence made him many enemies, and his hostility to the Howard connection finally turned even Carr against him. In 1613 he was offered his choice of diplomatic posts abroad, but refused. Not being able to get him out of the way by this means, Carr and the Howards had him committed to the Tower for disobedience. He was already ill at the time of his imprisonment in March, and his health gradually became worse; it is not clear how much of this was due to the poisoned jellies and tarts that the Countess of Essex was sending him, and how much to prison conditions. One of his letters to Carr during this time threatens to 'say something that you and I both repent'. He died on 15 September 1613, only ten days before the annulment of the Essex marriage. Apart from his sensational fate, he is best known as the author of a poem praising the ideal wife and a collection of characters and other short witty pieces, some of which were by other wits and courtiers of the period, including the dramatist John Webster, who also seems to have edited the collection. The characters sold very well even before the scandal broke, and inspired many imitators including Osborne. He seems to have been a misogynist, and may have been a homosexual, though report also linked his name with that of the Countess of Rutland. He was also thought to have written Carr's love letters to Lady Frances.

OWEN, John (1560?-1662). The author of numerous collections of epigrams (the first of which was published in 1606), but, since he wrote in Latin, more popular abroad than in England. His monument in St. Paul's became a favorite place for sticking verses and lampoons.

PACKER, John (1570-1649). He became secretary to Somerset in the latter's capacity as Lord Chamberlain in 1615, and when Buckingham succeeded Somerset Packer remained in the same office. He profited enormously under both Stuart kings, but in 1640 allied himself with Parliament, an act that was regarded as highly ungrateful.

PARSONS or Persons, Robert (1546-1610). In 1574, forced to resign his fellowship at Balliol for reasons which are still mysterious, he fled the country and, later that year, entered the Roman Catholic church at Louvain. He was ordained in 1578 and in 1580 he and Edmund Campion were sent in disguise on a mission to England where they made many converts. Campion was captured and executed in 1581 but Parsons fled back across the channel. This was the first of many intrigues designed to establish Catholicism in England. He was in overall charge of Jesuit missions to England from 1603, but accepted James's accession, and confined himself to controversial writing. He apparently knew nothing of the Gunpowder Plot of 1605, though many of those involved in it were his converts.

PEMBROKE: See William and Philip HERBERT, the third and fourth Earls of Pembroke.

Appendix

PERCY, Henry 9th Earl of Northumberland (1564-1632). Known as the 'Wizard Earl' because of his interest in science and the occult. After championing James's claim to the English crown in 1602-3, he was at first well rewarded, but he was soon disillusioned with the new regime. The Gunpowder Plot, in which his kinsman Thomas Percy was one of the ringleaders, made him an object of suspicion, and in 1606 Star Chamber sentenced him to life-imprisonment in the Tower. His release in 1621 was probably due to the intercession of his daughter's husband, James HAY. He was unhappy about this marriage, and also about that (in 1629) of his son Algernon 1602-1668 (later the 10th Earl) to a granddaughter of Robert CECIL: he claimed, Osborne says, that the blood of their two families 'would not mingle in a Bason' (Memoirs of King James, para. 20, p.68). Osborne may have known that the old earl wrote a book of advice to his son, when the latter was about to set off on his foreign travels. The 10th Earl held high office under Charles I but then took the side of Parliament; he seems to have been so respected a figure that he was able to continue in office even after the Restoration.

RADCLIFFE, Elizabeth, Lady Haddington (d. 1618). Daughter of the Earl of Sussex, married to John Ramsay, Viscount Haddington and Earl of Holderness (1580?-1626), who was a favorite of James's partly because he had killed the two leaders of the Gowrie conspiracy. Wilson says (History, p.12) that she was 'one of the prime Beauties of the Kingdom'. For their wedding in 1608 Jonson wrote his masque, The Hue and Cry After Cupid. Chamberlain quotes an example of her wit, directed against HAY, when the latter was about to set off in great pomp on an embassy to France: 'she sayes the flowre and bewtie of his embassage consists in three mignards, three daunsers, and three fooles or buffons' (Letters, II, p.14). After her death from smallpox in 1618, he wrote, 'howsoever she lived, [she] went away very virtuously' (II, p.193).

RALEGH, or Raleigh, Sir Walter (1552?-1618). Ralegh's career came to an end with the death of Queen Elizabeth. Henry HOWARD and others of his family had already been intriguing against him with the Scottish King. He was tried for treason in 1603, sentenced to death, but given a last-minute pardon which confined him to the Tower until he was released in 1616 to make his unsuccessful voyage to the new world. His estate at Sherborne was forfeited to CARR as a result of a legal error in the drafting of a document, a fact often alluded to in contemporary satires on the law. Osborne speaks admiringly of the History of the World,which Ralegh began in the Tower and left unfinished on the death of Prince Henry, and refers to his execution in 1618: 'His death was by him managed with so high and religious a resolution, as if a Roman had Acted a Christian, or rather a Christian a Roman ' (Memoirs of King James, para. 7).

RAMSAY. There were a good many Ramsays at the English court at the time of the Croyden incident in 1612, mentioned in I, i. The one who started the quarrel was William, or Patrick, Ramsay, the brother of Viscount Haddington. Chamberlain says that it nearly became a national quarrel, 'But for want of Weapons it was pacified' (Letters, I, p.340); the author of A Cat May Look Upon a King (p.49) thought that it had been planned with a view to massacring the English nobility if they had fought back; Osborne, in his Memoirs of King James, seems to think that the English refusal to fight was a national disgrace (para. 23-24). Ramsay was committed to the Tower after the King had personally enquired into the Croyden incident. He may have died in a brawl in 1615 - both combatants were named Ramsay, so it is difficult to be sure.

RI————, Lady. The 'most famous fair lady' whom Osborne describes as 'libidinous' may have been Penelope Devereux (1562?-1607), the sister of the 2nd Earl of Essex. She was married first to Lord Rich in 1581 and then, after her divorce from him in 1605, to her lover, the Earl of Mountjoy, by whom she had already had five children. She had been forced into marriage with Rich by her guardian, after having been engaged to Sir Philip Sidney, and neither she nor her many other admirers had any respect for her husband. Curiously, although Penelope and Mountjoy had lived in open adultery for years, their marriage, so soon after the divorce, led to disgrace for them both. The only other likely candidate for Osborne's dubious commendation might be the wife of RYCAUT mentioned in I, iv.

ROE, Sir Thomas (1581?-1644). A highly successful Jacobean diplomat who travelled extensively on government missions: up the Amazon in 1609-11, to India in 1614-18, to Turkey in 1621-28, Scandanavia in 1620, and Vienna in 1642. One of his most important contributions was the commercial treaty with the Great Mogul which was the foundation of British trade with India. He was also a scholar who brought important manuscripts back from his journeys; some of these are now in the Bodleian Library. Despite all this, he was

Appendix   151

not always paid promptly for his services and languished in
poverty for many years.

ROOS, or Ross, Lord: See William CECIL, Lord Roos.

RUDYERD, Sir Benjamin (1572-1658). A friend of Jonson, Owen,
Overbury, who was a fellow member of the Middle Temple, and
William Earl of Pembroke, with whom he collaborated on verses. By marriage he was allied to Lucy Countess of Bedford. He held a post in the Court of Wards and was, from
1620, a member of Parliament, where he was famous for his
eloquence. At first he tried to act as a mediator between
King and Commons, but he sided with Parliament in 1642, and
took the Covenant. In 1648 he tried again to urge accommodation with the king, was briefly imprisoned, and took no
further part in politics.

RUTLAND: See MANNERS.

RYCAUT or RICAUT, Sir Peter (d.1657?). A financier, the son
of a grandee from Brabant and a Spanish mother. He lent
money to kings of Spain and England, bought lands in England,
and was knighted by Charles I in 1641. He was finally
ruined by lending large sums to the royalist cause. His
youngest son Paul became a member of the Royal Society and
an expert on Turkey, of which he wrote a history. I do not
know whether this is the son whose wife Osborne describes in
I, iv.

SALISBURY: See Robert CECIL, Earl of Salisbury

SEYMOUR, Edward, Earl of Hertford (1539?-1621). As the son
of Edward Somerset, Protector of England under Edward VI,
who was executed in 1552, he was an object of suspicion to
Elizabeth and spent much of his youth in confinement. He
was in most danger when Elizabeth found out that he had secretly married Catherine Grey, the younger sister of Lady
Jane Grey and (by the terms of Henry VIII's will) the next
in line to the throne. Their two sons were born in the
Tower. The eldest, Edward Lord Beauchamp, was thought by
many to have a strong claim to succeed Elizabeth but was regarded as unfit; he died in 1612. Hertford himself - a
man of diminutive size who seems not to have inspired much
respect in his contemporaries - lived as quietly as possible
after his wife's death in 1568, though he did honor Elizabeth with a spectacular entertainment at Elvetham in 1591.
Both his second and third wives were named Frances Howard;

one, who died in 1598, was the daughter of William Lord
Howard of Effingham; for the other, see Frances HOWARD (2).
His marriage to her lacked banns or license and the preben-
dary who performed it was suspended. He was made Lord
Lieutenant of Somerset and Wiltshire in 1602, and lived much
of the rest of his life in that part of the country.
Osborne's account of his gravel walks sounds authentic, but
I have not been able to learn more about them.

SHIRLEY, Mrs. The name of the woman who supposedly took
Frances Howard's place in the examination to establish her
virginity is given differently by different authors. Weldon
says that it was a Mrs. Fiennes, and that he had the information from one who was in a position to know; Wilson says
merely that it was 'another young gentlewoman', and she is
said elsewhere to be a daughter of Sir Thomas Monson, who
later came under suspicion of being involved in the poisoning. Fiennes, Monson and Sir Thomas Shirley (one of the
famous Shirley brothers who made voyages to the east) had
daughters and were worried about money; this is probably
the only reason why their names were dragged into the story.
(See A.L. Rowse, Simon Forman, pp. 172-177 , for an account
of the dealings of Shirley and Monson with the astrologer.)

SIDNEY, Lady Barbara. Also known as Isabella, the daughter
of Robert Earl of Leicester. Chamberlain wrote of her marriage to 'young Tom Smith' in 1619: he 'is knowne to have
noe more mind to her then to any other woman, and perhaps
not so much.' (Letters, II, p.228). His great wealth, inherited from his father Sir Thomas SMITH, presumably made
him acceptable to her family.

SKELTON, John (1460?-1529). The famous poet of Henry VIII's
reign was remembered at the end of the century mainly as the
hero of a jestbook; he appears as a jester in The Downfall
of Robert Earl of Huntingdon (c. 1599) by Anthony Munday and
Henry Chettle.

SMITH/SMYTHE, Sir Thomas (c. 1558?-1625). Became wealthy in
his father's business as a haberdasher and rose to become
Governor of the East India Company, in 1600 and again from
1603-6 and 1607-1621, and Treasurer of the Virginia Company,
1609-1620. He also served as ambassador to Russia.

SOMERSET: Earl of Somerset: see Robert CARR. Countess of
Somerset: See Frances HOWARD (1)

Appendix

STONE, the Fool (d. 1606?). Little is known about this figure, mentioned as recently dead in Volpone, except two anecdotes. One is the insult to NOTTINGHAM (q.v.). The other, which seems related to it and which Osborne may also have known, is found in Selden's Table Talk (1689) and must have been around earlier: 'A gallant is above ill words. An example we have in the old lord of Salisbury, who was a great wise man. Stone had called some lord about court, fool, the lord complained, and has Stone whipped: Stone cries, I might have called my lord of Salisbury fool often enough, before he would have had me whipped.' (quoted in Ben Jonson, ed. Herford and Simpson, IX, p.701).

STUART, Lady Arabella (1575-1615). She was next after James himself in the line of succession to the Scottish throne, and the fact that she was born on English soil gave her, in the opinion of some, a better claim to the English one. James welcomed her to court at his accession, but in 1610 she made the mistake of a secret marriage to William Seymour, grandson of the Earl of Hertford, who was, like her, a possible claimant to the throne. James had them both arrested. They both tried to escape; he succeeded, but she was recaptured and committed to the Tower, where she died insane a few years later. After her death Seymour got permission to return to England and eventually married again.

STUART, Henry, Lord Darnley (1545-1567). The second husband of Mary Queen of Scots and father of James VI and I. As Osborne says, he was very good-looking, but he was also stupid and, by the end of his life, syphilitic as well. He was murdered in mysterious circumstances by an explosion at his house; Mary and her lover Bothwell were strongly suspected of having planned the murder. Recollections of the way in which his father died are supposed to have helped James to interpret the mysterious letter warning against the Gunpowder Plot.

STUART, Lodovick, 2nd Duke of Lennox and Richmond (1574-1624). JAMES's first favorite, while he was still a boy, was Esmé Stuart (1542?-1583), Lord Aubigny and 1st Duke of Lennox; he was forced by the Kirk to agree to his exile in 1583 and the Duke, on his deathbed, ordered that his heart should be sent to the young king as a sign of his devotion. Naturally, James was disposed to favor the son of this man, who was brought to court in the same year and, despite his youth, loaded with honors. These continued after 1603. He was a Gentleman of the Bedchamber and Privy Councillor, and his death was considered sufficient cause to postpone the opening of Parliament. Frances HOWARD (2) was his third wife. His brother, Esmé Stuart, 8th Lord Aubigny, was a patron of Jonson. Lennox's impressive physique, on which Osborne comments, is also described in a funeral elegy by Patrick Maguire:

> Thy comely looks, thy gesture, grace and gate[gait],
> Were such as well beseemed a man of State.
> No curious eye a blemish could impute
> To thy proportion, from the head to foot.

STUBBS, Katherine (1571-1590). The Puritan writer Philip Stubbs published in 1591 an immensely popular account of the short life of his wife Katherine, A Christal Glasse for Christian Women, which was still being reprinted as late as 1647. The narrative stresses her piety and exemplary death, which occurred as the result of a fever contracted shortly after childbirth.

SUFFOLK: see Thomas HOWARD, Earl of Suffolk.

TURNER, Anne (1576-1616). She was a Roman Catholic and a friend of the Suffolk family, particularly Frances. Her husband, George, had been a doctor; when he died in 1610 he virtually bequeathed her to Sir Arthur Mainwearing, whose mistress she had been for some time. She did not marry Sir Arthur but they continued to live together. Though she was thought to be the intermediary between FORMAN and Frances, there is (as A.L. Rowse notes) nothing about her in his papers. She had a patent for making yellow starch for ruffs. After her execution, they are said to have gone out of fashion, but Chamberlain mentions preachers inveighing against them several years later.

TYRONE: see Hugh O'NEILL, 2nd Earl of Tyrone.

UVEDALE, Lady. Presumably the wife of Sir William Uvedale/ Udall (c. 1585-1652), a follower of Carr's. He obtained the reversion of the post of Treasurer of the Chamber in place of OVERBURY, for whom Somerset had apparently intended it, and succeeded to the office in 1618. In the Civil War he sided with Parliament.

VILLIERS, George, 1st Duke of Buckingham (1592-1628). Born of an obscure family in Leicestershire , he owed his and his family's success entirely to the favor of James I. They met at Apthorp in 1614, and James took to him immediately, but Gardiner argues (II, 319-30) that it was Carr's folly

Appendix

rather than Villiers' ambition or the king's fickleness that
enabled the new favorite to rise at court. After the fall
of Somerset, he became Earl of Buckingham in 1617, Marquis
in 1619, and Duke in 1623, while he was in Madrid with
Prince Charles. Though at first he had the support of the
anti-Howard faction, the irresponsible way in which he used
his power for the aggrandisement of his family, many of
whom were Roman Catholics or suspected of a leaning to
Catholicism, soon made him intensely disliked. Shortly
after James's death, a rumor grew up that the Countess of
Buckingham, mother of the Duke, had poisoned the king.
Others said that the Duke himself had done so, fearing that
he might lose the king's favor and believing that his pros-
pects would be better under Charles. In 1626 George
Eglisham accused him in The Forerunner of Revenge, a pamphlet printed on the Continent, of having poisoned the
Marquis of HAMILTON in the previous year. Meanwhile, an
attempt to remove the Duke from office was ended only by
Charles's dissolution of Parliament. His sister, Susan,
the Countess of Denbigh, married her eldest daughter to
HAMILTON'S reluctant son; his mentally ill brother John
married Sir Edward COKE's daughter, despite her, and her
mother's, violent protests. Another two years, in which
Buckingham was virtually king of England, were finally ended
by the assassin John Felton, who had read the Remonstrance
of the House of Commons and the Eglisham pamphlet, and decided that Buckingham was a tyrant unfit to live. Some of
Charles's critics felt that his consistent defence of
Buckingham showed a lack of concern about the fate of his
own father. The favorite's death was the signal for universal rejoicing.

WEST, John. The man Osborne means is probably the one he
mentions in his Advice (part 2, para. 10) as Keeper of the
New Lodge at Barnet, and full of witty conceits. He was
apparently a member of the Mermaid Club, which included
wits and courtiers (see I.A. Shapiro's article on it, MLR
(1950), pp. 6-17).

WINDSOR, Thomas, 6th Baron Windsor (1591-1641). He was a
ward of the Earl of Northampton and, because his marriage
was childless, his barony fell into abeyance at his death.
Chamberlain reports that the astrologer John Lambe was
arraigned in about 1621 for 'bewitching my Lord Windsors
implement' (Letters, II, p.601).

WINWOOD, Sir Ralph (1563?-1617). A career diplomat, he first found favor at court under Essex, then Cecil, and had many diplomatic posts abroad. He was so willing to curry favor with the Somersets that, when Frances asked to borrow his horses for her coach after the wedding, he made her a present of them. Through the favorite's influence, he was appointed secretary of state in 1614. But when evidence of Overbury's murder came to his hands in 1615 he at once informed the king, and in 1616 he arranged for the trial of the Somersets. Naturally, there was much speculation about his motives for this action, but it seems unlikely that the crime could have been hidden in any case.

WOTTON, Sir Henry (1568-1639). A wit and scholar as well as a statesman; he was ambassador to Venice on several occasions, but finished his days as Provost of Eton, a post he held from 1624. (Northampton's account of him in I, v, conflates two widely separated episodes of his career.) In Overbury's Conceited News he was apparently expected to supply the foreign correspondence. He wrote a poem on the fall of Somerset, a panegyric on Charles I, and a parallel between Essex and Buckingham, first published in 1641. His collected works were published in 1651 as Reliquiae Wottonianae.

ZOUCH, Edward, Lord Zouche (1556?-1625). He lived on the Continent between 1587 and 1593, and was employed on a number of diplomatic missions in Elizabeth's time. He was a correspondent of Wotton's and a keen gardener; in his last years he held many important court posts.